ARABIC HISTORICAL PHRASEOLOGY

SUPPLEMENT TO

Written Arabic

AN APPROACH TO THE BASIC STRUCTURES

by

A. F. L. BEESTON

Laudian Professor of Arabic in the University of Oxford

CAMBRIDGE
AT THE UNIVERSITY PRESS
1969

Published by the Syndics of the Cambridge University Press
Bentley House, 200 Euston Road, London, N.W.1
American Branch: 32 East 57th Street, New York, N.Y. 10022

Library of Congress Catalogue Card Number: 68-29651
Standard Book Number: 521 09578 6

Printed in Great Britain
by Stephen Austin and Sons, Ltd., Hertford

CONTENTS

INTRODUCTION

The motivation behind this booklet is best explained by a quotation from the Introduction to Written Arabic: an approach to the basic structures: 'No exercise material is included, for two reasons. Firstly, there is the vocabulary problem. Arabic has a fundamental vocabulary of somewhere around a thousand words which will be essential for all users of the language; but above that level one begins to enter a sphere where the choice of requisite vocabulary is governed by the discipline in which the student is interested: many words which are basic for an economist will be useless for the historian, and vice versa. To insert exercise material adapted to any one discipline would vitiate the usefulness of the book to those concerned with another discipline. Ideally, what is needed is not one body of exercise material, but a set of parallel texts dealing with various subjects ... A second reason is that it is highly desirable that the student should at the earliest possible moment move on to work on the actual texts which he desires to read. While, therefore, a certain amount of 'illustrative' material additional to what is actually included here is no doubt desirable ... this should only be used to ensure comprehension of the principles enunciated in the book; the actual training in the application of those principles is preferably done by analysis of a chosen original Arabic work on the selected discipline, with constant reference back to this book, and with constant practice in the use of a dictionary'.

The present booklet, dealing with historical material, is designed as a first attempt towards fulfilling the need suggested in the foregoing quotation for a set of parallel 'illustrative' texts; it is hoped that others, dealing with other disciplines, may follow.

The sections here are adapted to the eighteen chapters of Written Arabic, and should be studied closely in connection with those chapters. The user is recommended to make sure that he fully understands, by reference to Written Arabic, the structure of the examples which illustrate that chapter. The translations given aim at being idiomatic, not literal, though a literal analysis is added in square brackets where this seems desirable; the idiomatic rendering which corresponds to the part so analysed runs either to the asterisk (where marked) or to the end of the example. While it is desirable that the user should study the examples with the help of the vocabularies, notes and dictionary before turning to the translations, he should not be discouraged if he does not always achieve a satisfactory rendering by this means, since many of the examples are designedly chosen to illustrate characteristic Arabic idioms and modes of expression.

The two main sources which have been drawn on for the examples are M.A. Enan's Decisive moments in the history of Islam (Cairo 1962), particularly the parts thereof dealing with the Crusades and with the Reconquista period in Spain; and the Memoirs on Egyptian Policy of M.H. Haykal (Cairo 1951), dealing with the political history of Egypt in the early decades of this century. It has, however, been necessary, specially in the earlier sections, to modify the phraseology in some cases, in order to avoid bringing the user into premature contact with features only dealt with at a later point in Written Arabic.

The following points should be noticed in connection with the Vocabularies:

1. In sections 3 onwards, only the commoner words are listed, which the student ought to memorize thoroughly. For other words he should gain practice in using Wehr's Dictionary of Modern Written Arabic; the notes afford any help likely to be necessary in identifying the root, or calling attention to any special peculiarity of the word-pattern. In sections 1 and 2 it has been necessary to give a vocabulary covering all the words used in the examples, but an asterisk denotes those which need not be memorized at this stage.

2. Verbs are shown in their perfect and imperfect, followed by the corresponding verbal abstract; the Roman figure after the rendering indicates the verb type, and the root is shown in brackets when not immediately obvious.

3. Nouns are shown in their singular form followed by the plural (when this is in use); as also are adjectives, when these have a 'broken' plural.

4. A generalized rendering is given in the vocabularies, though it will be appreciated that in a given context a different rendering (as given in the Translation) will often be idiomatically necessary in English.

5. Since the Vocabularies are intended to be memorized, they are not arranged alphabetically; the order of words is roughly that of occurrence in the examples. The index to the vocabularies will however enable the reader to refresh his

memory on any word. The index is arranged in dictionary style, with the words listed under their roots, but a few forms, of which the reader might find it difficult to trace the root, have been added in their alphabetical place.

6. The vocabularies include in principle only verbs, nouns and adjectives; it is expected that functionals will be learned from Written Arabic insofar as they are mentioned there. Apart from a few special cases, no derived adjectives (Written Arabic § 1:20) or intensified adjective forms (Ibid. § 10:1) are included, but only the basic noun or adjective as the case may be; the reader is expected to be able to associate the actually occurring pattern with the basic form cited in the vocabulary.

Since geographical and personal names often present a great stumbling block to the beginner, they are in these examples indicated by quotation marks (§ S:29), but it must be appreciated that Arabic printers will rarely do this except in the more unusual cases, which even an Arab might have difficulty in identifying. The mark of doubling (§ S:7) is consistently placed in the examples of sections 1 to 4, but thereafter only sporadically, as is the practice of Arabic printers.

VOCABULARIES AND NOTES

1

سَنَوات	سَنَة	year
أَعْوام	عام	year
قَلائِل	قَلِيل	few
	كَثِير	many
	كَثْرَة	frequency
أَخْطار	خَطَر	danger
	مُشْتَرَك	shared/common
فِكَر	فِكْرَة	idea
أَعْمال	عَمَل	deed/work/job
	عَمَلِيّ	practical
مَعارِك	مَعْرَكَة	battle/conflict
مَحالّ	مَحَلّ	locality
نَزَعات	نَزْعَة	tendency
	نِزاع	conflict/strife
أَدْيان	دِين	religion
	غَرْب	west
	شَرْق	east
عَساكِر	عَسْكَر	army

	ظَفَر	victory
	ظافِر	victorious
أُمَم	أُمّة	nation/people
	آخِر	last (feminine آخِرة)
	آخَر	other (feminine أُخْرَى)
آمال	أَمَل	hope
أَقْوام	قَوْم	folk/nation
	اِسْتِقْلال	independence
	مُسْتَقِلّ	independent
	خارِج	(noun) exterior
	داخِل	(noun) interior
	اِجْتِماع	society
	مُجْتَمَع	society
حُرُوب	حَرْب	war
حَمَلات	حَمْلة	campaign
	صَلِيب	*cross
	صَلِيبِيّ	Crusading/Crusader
مَمالِك	مَمْلَكة	kingdom/state
صِغار	صَغِير	small
كِبار	كَبِير	large
	أَخْلاق	(plural) morals/customs

طَبَقات	طَبَقَة	class
حُكّام	حاكِم	ruler
	حاكِم	ruling
	حُكْم	rule/regime/law
وَثائِق	وَثيقة	document
	مُهِمّ	important
	عالَم	world
	عامّ	(adjective) general
عَوامّ	عامّة	populace
رِجال	رَجُل	man
ناس	إِنْسان	human-being
أُمور	أَمْر	matter/affair
أَوامِر	أَمْر	command
أُمَراء	أَمير	prince/emir
إِمارات	إِمارة	principality/emirate
مَبادِئ	مَبْدَأ	start/origin/principle
	عِفاف	*decency
أَسْوار	سُور	wall
	تَسْليم	surrender
أَراضي	أَرْض	land/earth
	إِصْلاح	reform

أَحْوال	حال	state/condition/circumstance
تَوارِيخ	تَأْرِيخ	history
	حادِث	recent
	حَدَث	*young man
قُدَماء	قَدِيم	ancient (plural for persons only)
	حُرّ	free
مُدُن	مَدِينة	city
خُلَفاء	خَلِيفة	caliph
	خِلافة	caliphate
مَراكِز	مَرْكَز	centre
	جَدِيد	new
أَسْباب	سَبَب	cause
	ضَعِيف	weak
	ضُعْف	weakness
	طُلُوع	rise
	طالِع	(adjective) rising
	تَفَرُّق	disintegration
دُوَل	دَوْلة	state/realm/empire/dynasty
	وُجُود	existence
	وُجُوب	necessity
قُوّات/قُوَى	قُوّة	strength/force

	قَوِيّ	strong
	تَقْوِيَة	(noun) strengthening
طَوائِف	طائِفة	group
فُرْسان	فارِس	knight
أَفْراد	فَرْد	(noun) individual
	مَصْرَع	*debacle
	حَضارة	civilization
	ظِلّ	*shadow
	إِخْضاع	subjugation
خُطُوات	خُطْوة	step/measure/proceeding
	سابِق	preceding/precedent
أَشْباه	شِبْه	(noun) resemblance/like
جَزائِر	جَزِيرة	island
	شبه جزيرة	peninsula
قُوّاد/قادة	قائِد	commander
	عَقْد	(noun) tying up
مُعاهَدات	مُعاهَدة	treaty
	صُلْح	peace
	بَأْس	military strength
عَوامِل	عامِل	factor/agent
آثار	أَثَر	effect/consequence//monument

	شَدِيد	extreme/violent (plural of persons أَشِدَّاء ; of things شِدَاد)
	إِسْرَاف	*extravagance
تَدَابِير	تَدْبِير	plan/measure
قِصَار	قَصِير	short
آمَاد	أَمَد	term/limit
	خِبْرَة	experience/knowledge
	مُرّ	*bitter
شَكَاوِى	شَكْوَى	*complaint/grievance
	مَكَانَة	prestige
	سَيِّء	(adjective) evil
	عَظِيم	great/mighty (plural of persons عُظَمَاء ; of things عِظَام)
وَسَائِل	وَسِيلَة	means
	دِفَاع	defence
صُنُوف/أَصْنَاف	صِنْف	kind/variety
	مُقَاوَمَة	resistance/opposition
وَثَبَات	وَثْبَة	attack/onslaught
أَوْقَات	وَقْت	time
مَآزِق	مَأْزِق	crisis
حُصُون	حِصْن	fortress

أَجْنَبِيّ foreign/foreigner (plural of persons أَجانِب)

مُجاوِر neighbouring

Since in the case of the isolated phrases in this section there is no context to indicate whether a defined noun is being used as in § 1:1(a) or § 1:1(b), it may be said here that the renderings given for examples 4, 13, 15, 19, 25, 26, 74 assume the generalized use of definition, as described in § 1:1(b).

1. On these two alternative forms of expression see § 1:24, 25.

32. بَلَد with plural بِلاد means 'town'; but the form بِلاد is also used in the sense of 'country' or 'countries', while the plural form بُلْدان means only 'countries'.

45. The use of the annexion structure 'strengthening of the empire' is more fully explained in § 15:2.

53. On the breakdown of the centralized authority of the Abbasid caliphate in Baghdad, and of the Umayyad caliphate in Spain, effective power passed into the hands of localized rulers, who are commonly called 'the rulers of the groups'

68. طالع is here a noun which was used in mediaeval times for the 'ascendant star', i.e. the star which by

atrological ideas was though to govern the fate of a person or institution; in modern times it has come to be used for 'fate/luck'.

2

مَماليك	مَمْلُوك	slave/Mamluk
مُلُوك	مَلِك	king
	ظُلْم	tyranny/wrongdoing
	ظالِم	tyrannical
أَعْداء	عَدُوّ	enemy
	عُدْوان	enmity/agression
حَقائِق	حَقيقَة	truth/reality
	تَحْقيق	realization/ /investigation
غايات	غايَة	aim/terminal point
خَسائِر	خَسارَة	loss
وَقائِع	وَقيعَة	event/battle
أَمْثال	مِثْل	(noun) like
	حاسِم	decisive
	أَثْناء	duration/course (plural form)
	مُتَّصِل	continuous/adjacent
	وَحْدَة	unity

	بَرّ	land-mass/ shore
	ذَهاب	disappearance
	اسْتِرْداد	recovery
	رَغْم	spite
رِحَلات	رِحْلة	journey
نَتائِج	نَتيجة	result
أَبْحاث	بَحْث	research
سِياسات	سِياسة	policy
مُكاتَبات	مُكاتَبة	correspondence/ negotiation
أَبْواب	باب	gate/ / chapter
كُتُب	كِتاب	book
	إِفادة	information/ advantage
رِوايات	رِواية	account/ narrative
	زائِف	false
	صِحّة	health/ correctness/ truth
	صَحيح	true/ correct
	مُؤَرِّخ	historian
أَدْوار	دَوْر	phase/ / role
مَآسي	مَأْساة	*tragedy
أَرْواح	رُوح	spirit/ life
أَزْواج	زَوْج	spouse
بَنات	ابْنة	daughter

سَلاطين	سُلْطان	sultan/authority
	اسْتِحْمام	*bathing
	ضَرورة	necessity
أَقاليم	إِقْليم	climate/country
	حارّ	hot
آراء	رَأْي	view/opinion
	سائِد	prevalent
	إِعادة	renewal/repetition
	نَظَر	view
حَوائِج	حاجة	need
عَلاقات	عَلاقة	connection
	عِدّة	number
شُكوك	شَكّ	doubt
سَلاسِل	سِلْسِلة	series
مَصائِب	مُصيبة	disaster
	نَشْر	publication
بَرْقِيّات	بَرْقِيّة	telegram
	دَوِيّ	*echo
سِيَر	سِيرة	course/career
	اسْتراتيجيّ	*strategic

The first part of this section, comprising examples 1 to 40, consists of phrases only; the examples in the remainder are sentence structures.

46. It is not easy to give a satisfactory structural analysis of this sentence, because the correct analysis relies partly on the usage of an individual word: when آخَر is one of several qualificatives to a single noun, it normally occupies the last place; this excludes our analysing this speech segment as an entity-term phrase having the sense 'every other false account', and requires us to identify زائفة as a predicate. And although رواية is in a state of formal indefiniteness, the addition of 'every' to it gives it a logical definition, since it does not then admit (as does the simple undefined noun) uncertainty on the part of the hearer as to the precise individual concerned - all individuals of the category are envisaged; there is therefore at least a logical boundary of status between the theme-term 'every account' and the predicate 'false'. Finally, the reason why أخرى cannot be identified as a predicate resides in the nature of the concept of 'otherness': 'other' distinguishes one individual in a category from the remaining members of the category, and therefore

has no value as a communication predicating it of <u>every</u> member of the category.

67. Generalized definition of قائد العسكر , implying any and every such individual.

3

In this and the following vocabularies, verbs are listed together first, with nouns, adjectives and functionals afterwards.

أَمْر	يَأْمُرُ	أَمَرَ	command (ه) s.o. (ب) s.t. I
جَهْد	يَجْهَدُ	جَهَدَ	make an effort (فى) for s.t. I
إِرْسال	يُرْسِلُ	أَرْسَلَ	send (ه/ه) s.o./s.t. // send a message (ب) IV
شُعُور	يَشْعُرُ	شَعَرَ	feel (ب) s.t. I
خُرُوج	يَخْرُجُ	خَرَجَ	go outside/be outside (مِن) s.t. I
دُخُول	يَدْخُلُ	دَخَلَ	go inside/be inside (فى) s.t. I
قِيادة	يَقُودُ	قادَ	lead/command (ه) s.o. I
اِقْتِراب	يَقْتَرِبُ	اِقْتَرَبَ	approach (مِن) s.o./s.t. VIII
اِسْتِعْمال	يَسْتَعْمِلُ	اِسْتَعْمَلَ	use (ه) s.t. X
اِنْتِصار	يَنْتَصِرُ	اِنْتَصَرَ	gain victory (على) over s.o. VIII
هُجُوم	يَهْجُمُ	هَجَمَ	attack (على) s.o. I

اجْتَمَعَ يَجْتَمِعُ اجْتِماع	assemble//join (بِ) s.o. VIII
اشْتَرَكَ يَشْتَرِكُ اشْتِراك	participate (في) in s.t. VIII
قَدَّرَ يُقَدِّرُ تَقْدِير	estimate/appreciate (هـ) s.t. II
أَيَّدَ يُؤَيِّدُ تَأْيِيد	support (ه/هـ) s.o./s.t. II
ناسَبَ يُناسِبُ مُناسَبة	correspond/be appropriate (هـ) to s.t. III
عَبَّرَ يُعَبِّرُ تَعْبِير	express (عن) s.t. II
ثارَ يَثُورُ ثَوْر (ث و ر)	burst out/revolt I
أَثارَ يُثِيرُ إِثارة (ث و ر)	stir up/excite (ه/هـ) s.o./s.t. IV
تَكَلَّمَ يَتَكَلَّمُ تَكَلُّم	speak V
بَيَّنَ يُبَيِّنُ تَبْيِين	explain (هـ) s.t. II
تَشَكَّكَ يَتَشَكَّكُ تَشَكُّك	doubt (في) s.t. V
عادَ يَعُودُ عَوْدة (ع و د)	return I
جاءَ يَجِيءُ مَجِيء (ج ي ء)	come//bring (بِ) s.o./s.t. I
قامَ يَقُومُ قِيام (ق و م)	stand//perform (بِ) s.t. I
أَقامَ يُقِيمُ إِقامة (ق و م)	reside//set up (ه/هـ) s.o./s.t. IV
ماتَ يَمُوتُ مَوْت (م و ت)	die I
أَلْقَى يُلْقِي إِلْقاء (ل ق ي)	throw (ه/هـ) s.o./s.t. IV

جَرَى يَجْرِي جَرَيان (ج ر ي)	occur/proceed I
أَذاعَ يُذِيعُ إِذاعة (ذ ي ع)	publish/disseminate (ه) s.t. IV
اسْتَوْلَى يَسْتَوْلِي اسْتِيلاء (و ل ي)	control (على) s.o./s.t. X
أَجابَ يُجِيبُ إِجابة (ج و ب)	answer (ه) s.o. IV
أَوْجَبَ يُوجِبُ إِيجاب (و ج ب)	enjoin (ه) s.t. (على) on s.o. IV
اشْتَدَّ يَشْتَدُّ اشْتِداد	be/grow extreme VIII
صَحَّ يَصِحُّ صَحاح	be sound/correct/true I
عَمَّ يَعُمُّ عُمُوم	apply generally (ه/ه) to s.o./s.t. I
اسْتَمَرَّ يَسْتَمِرُّ اسْتِمْرار	be continuous X
اهْتَمَّ يَهْتَمُّ اهْتِمام	be concerned/interested (ب) in s.t. VIII
ظَهَرَ يَظْهَرُ ظُهُور	appear/emerge I
وَقَعَ يَقَعُ وُقُوع (و ق ع)	fall/occur I

مَجْهُود مَجْهُودات	effort
ماء مِياه	water
سائِر	(annexed) whole of//remainder of
سَفِينة سُفُن	ship
ساحِل سَواحِل	shore

أَسْلِحة	سِلاح	weapon
جُنُود	جُنْد	troops
مَصادِر	مَصْدَر	source
أَصْدِقاء	صَدِيق	friend
أَوْضاع	وَضْع	position
	ثَقافة	culture
قِصَص	قِصّة	story
	جُنُوب	south
	شَمال	north
نِساء	مَرْأة	woman
فُصُول	فَصْل	section/season
	خاصّ	particular/special (ب) to s.o./s.t.
نُفُوس/أَنْفُس	نَفْس	mind/self/soul/life
	مُقَدَّس	holy
	سِيادة	sovreignty
جُسُور	جِسْر	bridge
سُجُون	سِجْن	prison
بِحار/أَبْحُر	بَحْر	sea/lake
جَوانِب	جانِب	side/aspect
	بِضْعة	a small number

شُؤُون	شَأْن	affair//prestige
مَنَاشِير	مَنْشُور	proclamation
عِلَل	عِلَّة	malady//cause
قِلَاع	قَلْعَة	fortress
صُفُوف	صَفّ	rank
نَوَاحِي	نَاحِيَة	direction/region/aspect
	مُنْذُ / مُذْ	since
	كَ	as/like (§ S:4)

1. تَحْصِين verbal abstract II Type (root ح ص ن).

2. فَداحة noun of pattern فَعالة (ف د ح).

4. أُسْطُول 'fleet', a borrowing from Greek. سَيْطَرَ is a verb from a four consonant root, and has vowel patterns resembling those of a II Type verb.

10. فاجَأُوا III Type verb (ف ج ء).

11. قابَلْتَ III Type verb (ق ب ل).

16. انْفَجَرَ VII Type verb (ف ج ر). بُرْكان 'volcano', a borrowing from Latin.

19. تَرْتَكِز imperfect of VIII Type (ر ك ز).

20. يتناول imperfect of VI Type (ن و ل).

21. يتأهبون imperfect of VI Type (ء ه ب).

22. مهد noun of pattern فَعْل (م ه د).

26. تبالغ imperfect of III Type (ب ل غ).

31. برج a noun of pattern فُعْل

34. استرحت X Type verb (ر و ح), implying the theme pronoun 'I'.

35. ارتياع verbal abstract VIII Type (ر و ع).

37. تصفية verbal abstract II Type (ص ف و), see § 3:11 at end.

39. انهارت VII Type (ه و ر).

40. احتاطوا VIII Type (ح و ط).

41. نجت feminine of نجا (see § 3:27), I Type (ن ج و).

42. استولوا X Type, see vocabulary.

44. The spelling رآها deserves notice: the addition of the object pronoun entails the change of the spelling of $\bar{a}$ with ى into that with <u>alif</u> (§ 3:27), and this brings into play the spelling principle described in § S:20.

46. ارتدّ VIII Type (ر د د).

51. بثّ I Type verb (ب ث ث) here used in the sense 'spread/propagate'.

54. تضطرم VIII Type (ض ر م), see § 3:12(i).

56. أنساب plural of نَسَب 'genealogy'.

57. حاشِيَة noun of pattern فاعِلة (ح ش و).

61. See § 3:20.

62. اِضْمَحَلَّت verb from a four consonant root, having vowel patterns resembling those of a IX Type verb.

63. اِعْوِجاج verbal abstract IX Type (ع و ج).

4

اِتَّبَعَ يَتَّبِعُ اِتِّباع (ت ب ع)	follow (ه/هـ) s.o./s.t. VIII
أَرادَ يُرِيدُ إِرادَة (ر و د)	desire (هـ) s.t. IV
اِتَّصَلَ يَتَّصِلُ اِتِّصال (و ص ل)	be in contact (بـ) with s.o./s.t. VIII be continuous
قَدَّمَ يُقَدِّمُ تَقْدِيم	put forward (ه/هـ) s.o./s.t. II
تَقَدَّمَ يَتَقَدَّمُ تَقَدُّم	advance/progress V
أَصابَ يُصِيبُ إِصابَة (ص و ب)	hit/achieve (هـ) s.t./befall (ه) s.o. IV be right
أَبْدَى يُبْدِي إِبْداء (ب د و)	display (هـ) s.t. IV
بَدا يَبْدُو (ب د و)	appear I
اِسْتَفادَ يَسْتَفِيدُ اِسْتِفادَة (ف ي د)	gain advantage (بـ) from s.t. X

تَفَرَّقَ يَتَفَرَّقُ تَفَرُّق	disperse/disintegrate V	
رَجَعَ يَرْجِعُ رُجُوع	return/be referrable (إلى) to s.t. I	
رَاجَعَ يُرَاجِعُ مُرَاجَعَة	refer to/examine (ه/ـه) s.o./s.t. III	
اعْتَنَى يَعْتَنِي اعْتِنَاء (ع ن ى)	be concerned (ب) with s.t. VIII	
وَقَّعَ يُوَقِّعُ تَوْقِيع	sign (ـه) s.t. II	
صَرَفَ يَصْرِفُ صَرْف	turn (ه/ـه) s.o./s.t. I	
أَنْفَذَ يُنْفِذُ إِنْفَاذ	carry out (ـه) s.t. IV	
جَهَّزَ يُجَهِّزُ تَجْهِيز	equip (ـه) s.t. II	
وَجَّهَ يُوَجِّهُ تَوْجِيه	direct (ـه) s.t. II	
تَوَجَّهَ يَتَوَجَّهُ تَوَجُّه	direct oneself/move V	
نَشَأَ يَنْشَأُ نُشُوء/نَشْأَة	arise I	
اخْتَلَفَ يَخْتَلِفُ اخْتِلَاف	be different (من) from s.o./s.t. VIII	
	be various	
أَسَرَ يَأْسِرُ أَسْر	take prisoner/capture (ه) s.o. I	
انْتَبَهَ يَنْتَبِهُ انْتِبَاه	become aware (ل/إلى) of s.t. VIII	
أَدَّى يُؤَدِّي تَأْدِيَة (ء د ى)	lead (إلى) to s.t. II	

(ن م و) نما يَنمو نُمُوّ grow I

مَرَّ يَمُرّ مُرور pass (ب) through/by

اِسْتَمَرَّ يَسْتَمِرّ اِسْتِمْرار continue X

عارَضَ يُعارِض مُعارَضة oppose (ه/ه) s.o./s.t. III

حَوَّلَ يُحَوِّل تَحْويل change/convert/turn (ه) s.t. II

عَدِمَ يَعْدَم عَدَم lack (ه) s.t. I

قاوَمَ يُقاوِم مُقاوَمة resist (ه/ه) s.o./s.t. III

أَفْسَدَ يُفْسِد إِفْساد spoil/destroy (ه) s.t. IV

عَرَفَ يَعْرِف مَعْرِفة know/recognise (ه/ه) s.o./s.t. I

اِعْتَرَفَ يَعْتَرِف اِعْتِراف acknowledge (ب) s.o./s.t. VIII

(س و د) سادَ يَسُود سِيادة prevail I

مَنَحَ يَمْنَح مَنْح grant (ه) s.t. (ه) to s.o. I

تَطَوَّرَ يَتَطَوَّر تَطَوُّر develop V

رَسَمَ يَرْسُم رَسْم trace/prescribe (ه) s.t. I

أَمِنَ يَأْمَن أَمْن/أَمانة be secure (ه/ه) against s.o./s.t. I

(و ف ق) اِتَّفَقَ يَتَّفِق اِتِّفاق agree (ب) with s.o./s.t. VIII

طَلَبَ يَطْلُب طَلَب seek (ه/ه) s.o./s.t. I

فَعَلَ يَفْعَل فِعْل act/do (ه) s.t./deal (ب) with I

أَوْضَحَ يُوضِحُ إِيضَاح (وضح)	make plain (ه) s.t. IV
رَدَّ يَرُدُّ رَدّ	return/turn back I
نَجَحَ يَنْجَحُ نَجَاح	be successful I
سَعَى يَسْعَى سَعْي / مَسْعَى	strive/make an effort (لـ) for s.t. I
سَالَمَ يُسَالِمُ مُسَالَمَة	make peace (ه) with s.o. III
هَوِيَ يَهْوَى هَوَى	have a passion (ه/ه) for s.o./s.t. I
تَقَلَّبَ يَتَقَلَّبُ تَقَلُّب	move about V
اِرْتَبَطَ يَرْتَبِطُ اِرْتِبَاط	be tied (بـ) to s.o./s.t. VIII
أَخَذَ يَأْخُذُ أَخْذ	take (ه/ه) s.o./s.t. I
نَقَدَ يَنْقُدُ نَقْد	criticize (ه/ه) s.o./s.t. I
سَأَلَ يَسْأَلُ سُؤَال	ask (ه) s.o. (ه) for s.t. I
اِقْتَنَعَ يَقْتَنِعُ اِقْتِنَاع	be satisfied (بـ) with VIII
قَتَلَ يَقْتُلُ قَتْل	kill (ه) s.o. I
أَسْرَعَ يُسْرِعُ إِسْرَاع	hasten IV
اِبْن أَبْنَاء	son
مَوْقَعَة مَوَاقِع	battle
جِهَاد	(holy) war
مُنْتَظَم	organized

سُبُل	سَبِيل	way (feminine or masculine)
فِتَن	فِتْنة	discord/civil war
	عَزْمة	resoluteness
خَواطِر	خاطِر	mind/idea
جُيُوش	جَيْش	army
دِراسات	دِراسة	study
مَدارِس	مَدْرَسة	school
رُسُل	رَسُول	messenger
	واحِد	single
ظَواهِر	ظاهِرة	phenomenon
دَوافِع	دافِع	impulse/motive
ثَوْرات	ثَوْرة	revolt
أَزَمات	أَزْمة	crisis
عُلُوم	عِلْم	knowledge/science
نِيران	نار	fire
	صِراع	struggle
	مَشْرِق	east
عَناصِر	عُنْصُر	element
عُهُود	عَهْد	treaty//age/period
أَسْماء/أَسامِي	اسْم	name
	حُرِّيّة	freedom

مَوَاقِف	مَوْقِف	position
حُقُوق	حَقّ	truth//right/law
صُوَر	صُورَة	shape/appearance/picture
دَسَاتِير	دُسْتُور	constitution
رَوَابِط	رَابِطَة	tie/bond
أَوْطَان	وَطَن	homeland
أَضْوَاء	ضَوْء	light
	عِنَايَة	care/attention
	مَبْلَغ	quantity/amount
وُفُود	وَفْد	delegation/deputation
	حَظّ	share/lot/luck
بِقَاع	بُقْعَة	area of land
	وَرَاءَ	beyond
	أَمَامَ	in front of

Examples 1 to 7 in this section are entity-term phrases, the remainder are sentence structures.

1. See § S:27(iii).
2. خطورة noun of pattern فُعُولة (خ ط ر).
4. شهرته feminine perfect of I Type with object pronoun.
5. أحرزته feminine perfect of IV Type (ح ر ز) with object pronoun.

6. دمار noun of pattern فِعال (د م ر).

7. براعة noun of pattern فَعالة (ب ر ع).

8. تحجّب verbal abstract V Type.

9. مُراعاة verbal abstract III Type (ر ع ى).

11. جالت feminine perfect I Type (ج و ل).

13. جُذُور plural of جِذْر 'root'.

14. See note to section 3, ex. 54.

15. أَوْفَدَ pefect of IV Type (و ف د). يُنْذِر imperfect of IV Type (ن ذ ر).

16. أَسْر verbal abstract of I Type (ء س ر).

17. ذَوْد verbal abstract of I Type (ذ و د).

18. تجلب feminine imperfect I Type.

21. شامل 'general/universal'. بَيِّن 'evident'.

23. أَذْكَتْ feminine perfect IV Type (ذ ك و).

24. حماسة noun of pattern فَعالة (ح م س).

27. خالِق 'Creator'.

28. See notes to section 3, exx. 16 and 54.

30. إِرْهاق verbal abstract IV Type. مُنْشِئ noun of pattern مُفْعِل (ن ش ء).

31. تكفل feminine imperfect I Type.

32. مَخاوِف plural of مَخافة (خ و ف). مَعْقِل noun of pattern مَفْعِل (ع ق ل).

33. اتّفاقيّة is a noun evolved by the addition of -iyya (see 1:22) to the verbal abstract اتّفاق VIII Type (و ف ق), from which it differs in sense only by a narrow margin, not reproducible in English; effectively, both have to be rendered by 'agreement'.

35. أسلاف plural of سَلَف 'ancestors/forebears'.

40. تنطوى feminine imperfect VII Type (ط و ى).

41. يقتضى imperfect VIII Type (ق ض ى).

42. تلويح verbal abstract II Type (ل و ح).

43. أضناهم perfect of IV Type (ض ن ى) with object pronoun.

45. عاتق noun of pattern فاعِل

46. أقوات plural of قوت 'foodstuff'.

49. الوفد is the name adopted by a party influential in Egypt in the twenties and thirties of this century.

5/6

تَرَكَ يَتْرُكُ تَرْك leave/let alone (ه/ه) s.o. /s.t. I

أَرَى يُرِى show (ه ه) s.o. s.t. IV

[§ 3:12(i)]

رَمَى يَرْمِى رَمْى aim at (ه/ه/إلى) s.o. /s.t. I

قَضَى يَقْضِي قَضاء — accomplish (ھ) s.t./put an end (على) to s.o./s.t. I

وَقَفَ يَقِفُ وُقُوف — stand//comprehend (على) s.t. I

أَعْوَزَ يُعْوِزُ إِعْواز — be lacking to (ه/ھ) s.o./s.t. IV

كَتَبَ يَكْتُبُ كِتابة — write (ھ) s.t. I

دَفَعَ يَدْفَعُ دَفْع — push/repel/impel (ه) s.o.//motivate (إلى) s.t.//defend (عن) s.o.//pay (ھ) s.t. I

عَنَى يَعْنِي عِنايَة/مَعْنًى — mean (ھ) s.t./concern (ه) s.o. I

حَدَثَ يَحْدُثُ حُدُوث — occur I

فَسَّرَ يُفَسِّرُ تفسير — explain (ھ) s.t. II

عَزَمَ يَعْزِمُ عَزْم — resolve (على) on s.t. I

غادر يغادر مغادرة — leave/abandon (ه/ھ) s.o./s.t. III

استطاع يستطيع استطاعة — be able to do (ھ) s.t. X

فَهِمَ يَفْهَمُ فَهْم — understand (ه/ھ) s.o./s.t. I

ضَرَبَ يَضْرِبُ ضَرْب/ضَرْبَة — strike (ه/ھ) s.o./s.t. I

لَقِيَ يَلْقَى لِقاء — meet (ه/ھ) s.o./s.t. I

انْتَهَى يَنْتَهِي انْتِهاء (ن ه ي) come to an end VIII

فاوَضَ يُفاوِض مُفاوَضة negotiate (ه) with s.o. III

أَفْرَجَ يُفْرِج إِفْراج release (عن) s.o. IV

وَعَدَ يَعِد وَعْد (و ع د) promise/threaten (ه) s.o. (ب) s.t. I

أَيْقَنَ يُوقِن إِيقان (ي ق ن) be certain (ه) of s.t. IV

وَصَلَ يَصِل وُصُول arrive I

امْتازَ يَمْتاز امْتِياز (م ي ز) be characterized (ب) by s.t.; excel (على) s.o. VIII

ضَمَّ يَضُمّ ضَمّ join (ه/ه) s.o./s.t. (إلى) to s.o./s.t.; include (ه/ه) s.o./s.t. I

ذَكَرَ يَذْكُر ذِكْر mention/remember (ه/ه) s.o./s.t. I

اعْتَقَدَ يَعْتَقِد اعْتِقاد believe (ه) s.t. VIII

أَنْزَلَ يُنْزِل إِنْزال let fall (ه) s.t.; settle (ه) s.o. IV

تَصَرَّفَ يَتَصَرَّف تَصَرُّف behave/conduct oneself V

ضَرَّ يَضُرّ ضَرّ harm (ه/ه) s.o./s.t. I

أَمْكَنَ يُمْكِن إِمْكان be possible (ه) to s.o. IV

اعْتَدَلَ يَعْتَدِل اعْتِدال	be moderate VIII
تَعَسَّرَ يَتَعَسَّر تَعَسُّر	be difficult/be impossible V
قَصَدَ يَقْصِد قَصْد	aim (إلى/ه) at s.t. I
أَدارَ يُدِير إِدارة (دور)	direct/administer (ه) s.t. IV
اخْتَصَّ يَخْتَصّ اخْتِصاص	be special (ب) to s.o. be specially concerned (ب) with s.t. VIII

	صَعْب	difficult
	صُعُوبة	difficulty
	دَعْوة	propaganda/cause
	نَهْضة	revival
	طَيِّب	good
سُلْطات	سُلْطة	authority
	عَظَمة	greatness
أَصْحاب	صاحِب	companion/possessor
حُجَج	حُجّة	argument/proof
نُوّاب	نائِب	lieutenant/deputy
أَهالي	أَهْل	populace/people
	أَمان	immunity/safe-conduct
رُؤَساء	رَئِيس	chief

وزارات	وِزارة	ministry
مناصب	مَنْصَب	office
دلائل	دَلالة	indication
قرارات	قَرار	decision
نظريّات	نَظَرِيّة	theory
	أكثريّة	majority
أخبار	خَبَر	information
	ظاهِر	manifest
فُرَص	فُرْصة	opportunity
وَفَيات	وَفاة	death
	نِسْبة	relation/ comparison
مَخارِج	مَخْرَج	way out
	وَحيد	sole/unique
	مُسَلَّح	armed
	أَهَمِّيّة	importance
	كَيْفَ	how

1. ثِياب plural of ثَوْب 'garment'.

2. The final member of this sentence, in which لسحقّ can only be analyzed as preposition <u>li-</u> with verbal abstract سَحْق, shows that لبث is similarly to be analyzed as verbal abstract بثّ (note to section 3, ex. 51) with preposition, and is not to be regarded as deriving from the root ل ب ث

3. The final alifs denote the object status of خطر after لكنّ , see §3:29, §6:3(i, iii).

4. The initial l before بِشارة 'good news' here represents la, see §6:3(i).

6. جئنَ feminine perfect I Type (ج ي ء).

7. جَواسيس plural of جاسُوس 'spy'. خَوَنة plural of خائِن 'traitor', (خ و ن). مَخاوف plural of مَخافة (خ و ف).

9. Note the structure in which the agent of the verb is not identical with the theme term; other examples will be met with later.

11. The I Type verb قَدِمَ يَقْدَمُ قُدُومٌ when followed by بِ has the same sense as the II Type قدّم with direct object (Vocabulary 4).

12. تَعَصُّب verbal abstract of V Type.

15. The noun رَدّ when annexed often serves as the equivalent of the English prefix 're-'.

20. تُحجِم imperfect of IV Type (ح ج م).

22. مُلِحّ adjective, 'urgent/pressing' (ل ح ح). اتّجاه has the pattern of a VIII Type verbal abstract (و ج ه), but is also employed as a noun, 'trend'.

23. كَفِيل is an adjective meaning 'guaranteeing' (بِ) s.t.;

in English idiom, however, it is customary to say that someone or something 'is guaranteed to' rather than 'is guaranteeing'. أُهْبَة noun (ء ه ب).

24. The two parallel members have here been differently expressed, the first by a verbal abstract, the second by a noun-clause (with omission of the pronoun, §6:6), for rhetorical variation.

25. أَبَتْ feminine perfect I Type (ء ب ى). وَفَاء noun from root و ف ى

33. اِسْتَغَلُّوا X Type (غ ل ل).

40. شارلكان represents the French form 'Charles Quint'.

41. تلجأ feminine imperfect I Type.

43. حُسْن I Type verbal abstract, 'goodness'.

44. مُسْتَنِير adjective (ن و ر).

45. بَيْت المَقْدِس ('house of the holy') is the ordinary mediaeval designation of Jerusalem; in modern usage it is القُدْس ('holiness').

46. إِذًا see §S:27(ii). مُلْزِم adjective (ل ز م).

7

شاءَ يَشاء مَشِيئة (ش ي ء)	wish/will (ه) s.t. I
أعادَ يُعيد إعادة (ع و د)	renew/restore/do again (ه) s.t. IV
نَسِيَ يَنْسَى نِسْيان	forget (ه/ه) s.o./s.t. I
أَصْدَرَ يُصْدِر إصْدار	issue (ه) s.t. IV
حَلَّ يَحُلّ حَلّ	loose (ه) s.t. I
حَلَّ يَحِلّ حُلُول	settle (ب) in/at I

مُهِمَّة مُهِمّات	business
حِياد	neutrality
قَدَر	(divine) decree/fate
قاهِر	conqueror
مَجْلِس مَجالِس	council
أَسِير أَسْرَى	prisoner
مُعْظَم	greater part
قاعِدة قَواعِد	base
قاضي قُضاة	judge/magistrate
فَتْرة فَتَرات	space of time
بَلِيغ	far-reaching
طَبْع	nature

مَساكين مِسْكين poor

سادة سَيِّد master/lord/chieftain

1. ساسة plural of سائس, noun from root س و س

2. ضحايا plural of ضَحِيّة (ض ح ى); this is the beginning of the predicate, the marker pronoun being here omitted, see §2:8.

5. بَطَل is a noun belonging to the second of the roots listed by Wehr under ب ط ل .

7. أَسرى plural of أسير (ء س ر).

8. Cp section 5/6, ex. 37.

9. اقتطاع verbal abstract VIII Type, is a technical term of mediaeval history meaning occupation by feudal tenure; parallel to it is the IV Type verb أَقْطَعَ يُقْطِع إِقطاع with direct personal object, meaning 'grant a feudal tenure to s.o.'

10. انهيار verbal abstract VIII Type (ه و ر).

12. دسائس plural of دَسِيسة (د س س).

17. مَغْنَم noun from root غ ن م . For the idiomatic use of من وراء see Wehr under the preposition وراء listed under root و ر ى .

20. مَدْيُونِيّة noun from the first root listed in Wehr under د ى ن . إِنكار الجميل literally 'denial of benefit' is idiomatic for 'ingratitude'. In this example cp. § 2:15.

21. Cp section 2, ex. 57.

22. نظائع plural of نظاعة (ن ظ ع).

25. غدا يغدو is another of the verbs which modify the basic thematic sentence by the addition of the concept 'begin'.

26. تنافس feminine imperfect III Type (ن ف س).

8

أخرج يخرج إخراج	expel/send out (ه/ه) s.o./s.t. IV
اضطر يضطر اضطرار (ض ر ر)	compel (ه) s.o. (على) to s.t. VIII
استسلم يستسلم استسلام	surrender oneself X
أسند يسند إسناد	entrust (ه) s.t. (إلى) to s.o. IV
أخلى يخلي إخلاء (خ ل و)	empty (ه) s.t. IV
وجد يوجد وجود	be found/exist I (vague)
فقد يفقد فقدان	lose (ه/ه) s.o./s.t. I
دعا يدعو دعاء (د ع و)	call (ه) s.o. (بـ/ه) s.t. I
استقال يستقيل استقالة	resign X
ألف يؤلف تأليف	compose (ه) s.t. II
تذكر يتذكر تذكر	remember (ه) s.t. V
أباح يبيح إباحة (ب و ح)	allow/permit (ل) s.o. (ه) to do s.t. IV

زاد يزيد زيادة (ز ي د)	increase (ه) s.t. I
تظاهر يتظاهر تظاهر	stage a demonstration VI
دلّ يدلّ دلال	indicate/demonstrate (على) s.t. I
أقنع يقنع إقناع	convince (ه) s.o. (على) of s.t. IV
انبغى ينبغي (ب غ ي)	be suitable/appropriate VII
نجا ينجو نجاة (ن ج و)	escape I
أجمع يجمع إجماع	generally consent (على) to s.t. IV
اتّهم يتّهم اتّهام (و ه م)	suspect (ه/ه) s.o./s.t. (ب) of s.t. VIII
مال يميل ميل	incline/tend I
اعتزل يعتزل اعتزال	retire VIII
محكمة محاكم	court
جوار	neighbourhood
معسكر معسكرات	camp
مقصد مقاصد	aim/objective
رسميّ	official
مساحة	area/extent
دم دماء	blood
مال أموال	wealth/property

A considerable number of words having a participle pattern have already been cited in the earlier vocabularies, and the reader is advised to go through them identifying these; only a few examples are given here.

1. المخالف participle of III Type, with article denoting generalized definition.

3. عيال plural of عَيِّل (ع و ل).

5. Zallaqa, near Badajoz, was the scene of an important battle between the Almoravid leader Yusuf ibn Tashfin and Alphonso VI.

9. أخذ followed by على and a personal object, with non-personal direct object, means 'criticize s. o. for s.t.'; in the form of vague application, therefore, it is the 'thing' which functions as surrogate agent, contrary to English usage.

10. Omission of pronoun before أَنَّ, § 6:6.

15. Cp section 4, ex. 34.

16. قَتْلَى plural of قتيل a noun having the same sense as the participle form مَقْتُول. Cp also note to section 7, ex. 7.

18. خوطب vague form perfect of III Type خاطب

19. This example illustrates the use of واقعة as an adjectival participle, and not in the specialized noun use of 'battle/event' which it also has.

21. كَنِيسة 'church'.

24. سالَت feminine perfect I Type (س ي ل).

25. This structure is generated from (a) عَبَّرْتُ عن الفكرة 'I expressed the idea', (b) عُبِّرَ عن الفكرة 'the idea was expressed'.

26. Structure generated in the same way as above.

27. Generated from (a) اتّفقوا على سياسة 'they agreed on a policy', (b) اتُّفِقَ على سياسة 'a policy was agreed on'.

28. Equivalent to الخليفة الذى زُعِمَ أنّه نجا

29. Equivalent to شيخا يُجمَع على خبرته

30. Equivalent to مِثل هذا... . وزير يُتّهم تدبيره 'the like of this ...' is the normal Arabic structure corresponding to English 'such a ...'

9

(د و م) دام يدوم دوام continue I

(ز و ل) زال يزال زوال cease I

متابعة يتابع تابَعَ follow/pursue (ه/ه) s.o./s.t. III

مَنَعَ يَمْنَعُ مَنْع	prevent (ه/ه) s.o./s.t. I
مَضَى يَمْضِي مُضِيّ	go/pass/elapse I
وَضَعَ يَضَعُ وَضْع	put/place/set down (ه) s.t. I
أدامَ يُدِيم إدامة (دوم)	lengthen (ه) s.t. IV
اكْتَفَى يَكْتَفِي اكتفاء (كفي)	be content (ب) with s.t. VIII
ظَنَّ يَظُنُّ ظَنّ	think (ه) s.t. I
قاتل يقاتل مقاتلة	fight (ه) s.o. III
واجه يواجه مواجهة	confront/combat (ه/ه) s.o./s.t. III
حَصَلَ يَحْصُل حُصُول	result//achieve (على) s.t. I
طال يطول طُول	be long I
خلا يخلو خُلُوّ	be void I
سار يسير سَيْر/مَسِير	travel/go/march I
قَوِيَ يَقْوَى قُوّة	be strong I
تعذّر يتعذّر تعذّر	be difficult/impossible (على) for s.o. V
قال يقول قَوْل	say (ه) s.t. I
اتّسع يتّسع اتّساع (وسع)	be ample VIII
فصّل يفصّل تفصيل	divide/detail (ه) s.t. II
تواصل يتواصل تواصل	come uninterruptedly VI
انتظر ينتظر انتظار	expect/wait for (ه/ه) s.o./s.t. VIII

بَنَى يَبْنِي بِناء	build (ه) s.t. I
قَبِلَ يَقْبَل قُبُول	accept (ه) s.t. I
صرّح يصرّح تصريح	declare (ب) s.t. II
أعلن يعلن إعلان	announce (ه) s.t. IV

خِلاف خِلافات	dispute/ controversy/ dissension
بَقِيّة	remainder
خَطّ خُطُوط	line
عُمْر أعْمار	life
مَرَض أمْراض	sickness
نِيّة نَوايا	intention (ن و ى)
أَهْل	fit/ suitable (ل) for
لَجْنة لَجَنات	committee
عَدَد	number
مَعْنًى مَعانِي	meaning
طَوْر أطْوار	phase
شِدّة	violence/ extremeness
مَقام مَقامات	place/ space
نِصْف	half
قَرْن قُرُون	age/ century
شَخْص أشْخاص	person

أحيان حِين time

فَوْر present/immediate moment

1. مندوب participle cf مفعول pattern (§ 8:11), used also as a noun with specialized sense 'commissioner'. سامي participle pattern فاعل (§ 8:7) from root س م و .

6. The verb لَبِثَ when negatived and followed by أَنْ has the idiomatic sense of 'not be long before doing s.t.'

7. برنامج 'programme' is of Persian origin.

8. تقاليد plural of تقليد, a noun having the pattern of a verbal abstract of II Type. ماضي participle pattern فاعي (م ض ى) used as noun with the specialized sense 'the past'.

10. نِضال noun (ن ض ل). بُطُولة noun from the second root listed in Wehr under ب ط ل .

12. حَوْل and طَوْل are synonyms both meaning 'power', and the use of the two together for emphasis is a linguistic cliché of a kind which may not infrequently be met.

14. يَفِرّ imperfect I Type (ف ر ر).

15. See § 2:18.

20. متنابذ participle pattern VI Type (ن ب ذ).

21. عهد and ذمام together constitute a pair (cp note to ex. 12 above) meaning 'sense of honour/obligation'. أهل للوفاء

means strictly 'the sort of person likely to fulfil his obligations' (cp. section 5/6, ex. 25).

22. أعضاء plural of عُضْو 'member'.

23. مؤلّف participle pattern of II Type verb (see vocabulary to section 8), used in the sense of 'compose (a book)', hence 'author'.

25. تملأ imperfect I Type (م ل ء).

30. Cp section 8, ex. 9 and note thereto.

31. Cp section 8, ex. 21.

32. Cp section 5/6, ex. 20.

33. مبعث noun (ب ع ث).

35. فِقْه is the technical term for Islamic jurisprudence, but is also used more generally for any organized body of learning (e.g. grammar etc.).

37. إمدادات plural of verbal abstract IV Type (م د د).

38. تعاون verbal abstract VI Type (ع و ن).

10

شَهِدَ يَشْهَدُ شَهادة witness (ب/ه) s.t. I

رَوَى يَرْوِي رِواية relate (ه) s.t. I

وَصَفَ يَصِفُ وَصْف describe (ه/ه) s.o./s.t. I

complete (ه) s.t. IV	أَتَمَّ	يُتِمُّ	إِتْمام
conquer/gain control (بِ) of s.t. I	ظَفِرَ	يَظْفَرُ	ظَفَر
stipulate/impose a condition (ه) I	شَرَطَ	يَشْرُطُ	شَرْط
be weak I	ضَعُفَ	يَضْعُفُ	ضُعْف
begin I	بَدَأَ	يَبْدَأُ	بَدْأ
name (ه) s.o. (بِ) s.t. II	سَمَّى	يُسَمِّي	تَسْمِية
good (§ 10:11)	خَيْر	أَخْيار	
bad (§ 10:11)	شَرّ	أَشْرار	
brave	شُجاع	شُجْعان	
ugly/horrid	شَنيع		
beautiful	جَميل		
house (feminine)	دار	دُور	
library	دار الكُتُب		
frontier	ثَغْر	ثُغُور	
harm/damage	أَذًى		
error/mistake	خَطَأ	أَخْطاء	
fact	واقِع		
remote/far	قَصِيّ		

	فَقْر	poverty
حُدُود	حَدّ	limit/boundary
	رَدِيء	base/vile
سَلْطَنات	سَلْطَنة	sultanate
عُصُور	عَصْر	age
	شِعْر	poetry
	واسِع	extensive
	مَدًى	extent/limit
	كَما	as

1. اجتاحوا perfect of VIII Type (ج و ح). أَقَلّ intensified form of the adjective قَليل (vocabulary 1).

2. أَنْكَى intensified adjective pattern, root ن ك ى , the simple adjective being not in use.

4. اضطرام see note to section 3, ex. 54. Whereas English disposes of the alternative structures 'weaker than in the east' and 'weaker than it was in the east', the normal Arabic structure is 'weaker than it in the east'.

7. أَبْطال plural of بَطَل 'hero'.

9. آثار plural of أَثَر (vocabulary 1).

10. أَنْأَى intensified pattern to نائي 'remote', a participle of فاعل pattern (ن ء ى).

11. أَرْوَعُ is recorded in Wehr only as an intensified pattern to رائِع 'charming/magnificent', but is here employed as intensive pattern to مُرَوِّع 'terrible' (root روع in both cases).

13. جَرائِم plural of جَرِيمة 'crime'.

14. أَحَقّ followed by بـ serves as intensified pattern to مستحقّ 'worthy/entitled/deserving'.

15. أَمَسّ intensified pattern to ماسّ , an adjective of فاعِل pattern from root م س س , and a cliché in connection with the noun حاجة ماسّة 'urgent need'.

16. The two adjectives are both annexed (§ 5:8).

21. سُهُول plural of the noun سَهْل

23. أَسْوَأ intensified pattern to سَيِّء

26. فُلُوس plural of فِلْس , a coin of small value; in modern Iraq it has been used to denote the one-hundredth part of a dinar.

34. أَهَمّ intensified pattern to هامّ 'important'. اعتنت feminine pefect VIII Type (ع ن ى), cp. vocabulary 4.

35. شعوبية is an abstract (§ 1:22) formed from شُعُوب 'nations', and is sometimes used generally in the sense of 'nationalism', but much more frequently as a technical term

for the anti-Arab feeling which manifested itself among the Muslim populations of Iranian stock in the beginning of the Abbasid regime.

37. أَشَدّ intensified pattern to شديد

11

تحرّك	يتحرّك	تحرُّك	move V
ارتدّ	يرتدّ	ارتداد	retire/go back VIII
أدرك	يدرك	إدراك	reach (ه/ھ) s.o./s.t. // comprehend (ھ) s.t. IV
خَضَعَ	يَخْضَع	خُضُوع	submit I
أَسَرَ	يَأْسِر	أَسْر	take prisoner/capture (ه) s.o. I
ذاع	يذيع	ذُيُوع	spread/become known I
وحّد	يوحّد	توحيد	unite (ه/ھ) s.o./s.t. II

مَكان	أَمْكِنَة	place
جِهة	جِهات	direction/quarter
سَفِير	سُفَراء	ambassador
شَهْر	شُهُور / أَشْهُر	month
شُهْرَة		fame

أَوْسَاط	وَسْط	middle part
مِرَار/مَرَّات	مَرَّة	time/occasion
غُزَاة	غَازٍى	raider
مُقَدِّمَات	مُقَدِّمَة	forefront/preface
	ضَخْم	large
	مَرِيض	sick
أُسُس	أَسَاس	basis
	نَحْوَ	towards
/إِزَاءَ	حِذَاءَ	opposite
	هٰكَذَا	thus

3. انساب perfect VII Type (س ى ب). سهول see note to section 10, ex. 21.

4. يتحيّن imperfect V Type (ح ى ن). مشروع is a participle pattern مفعول, but used as a noun with specialized sense 'scheme/plan/project'.

5. من قبل corresponds to the French 'de la part de'.

6. السيل generalized definition, since 'any and every torrent' is intended. مَن see § 4:6.

11. سيحرث see § 3:21.

15. حيّاني perfect of II Type (ح ى و) with object pronoun added. ابتسامة the termination -a(t) is sometimes added to a

verbal abstract pattern (here بـس ٣ VIII Type) conveying the idea of a single occurrence, or a variety, of the action, as distinct from the action considered purely abstractly.

17. بيت المقدس see note to section 5/6, ex. 45.

19. بايع with direct personal object is a III Type verb (ب ى ع) meaning 'make a contract with s.o.', but is also employed as a technical term for swearing allegiance (particularly to a caliph), owing to the contractual notion underlying that procedure. ثُوّار plural of ثائر a participle pattern فاعل from root ث و ر (§ 8:8), the verb being ثار (vocabulary 3).

20. مِحَفّة noun from root ح ف ف .

22. عُزْل plural of أَعْزَل , see § 10:14.

23. وَحْدَ annexed to a pronoun means 'alone/by oneself'.

12

تبيّن	يتبيّن	تبيّن	become clear/see (ﻫ) s.t. clearly V
تطبيق	يطبّق	طبّق	apply (ﻫ) s.t. (على) to s.t. II
نَظَر	يَنْظُر	نَظَرَ	look (ﻫ/إلى) at s.t. I
إنذار	ينذر	أنذر	warn (ه) s.o. IV

نِسْبة	يَنْسُبُ	نَسَبَ	attribute (إلى) s.t. (ه) to s.o. I
محالفة	يحالف	حالف	ally oneself (ه) with s.o. III
مبالغة	يبالغ	بالغ	exaggerate (في) s.t. III
توكيل	يوكّل	وكّل	authorize (ه) s.o. II
كَفالة	يَكْفُل	كَفَلَ	guarantee (ه) s.t. (ل) to s.o. I
احتشاد	يحتشد	احتشد	gather together/rally VIII
سُلُوك	يَسْلُك	سَلَكَ	go/travel (ه) along s.t. I
وَسْع	يَسَع	وَسِعَ	be large enough (ه) for s.t. / be within the power (ه) of s.o. I
اتّحاد (وحد)	يتّحد	اتّحد	be united VIII
حَمْل	يَحْمِل	حَمَلَ	carry I
حِماية	يَحْمِي	حَمَى	protect (ه/ه) s.o./s.t. I
اختلاط	يختلط	اختلط	be confused/mixed VIII
تحوُّل	يتحوّل	تحوّل	be changed/altered V
اتّجاه (وجه)	يتّجه	اتّجه	tend (إلى) towards s.t. VIII
ازدياد (زيد)	يزداد	ازداد	increase VIII
حِسْبان	يَحْسُب	حَسِبَ	think/reckon I
اشتراك	يشترك	اشترك	participate (في) in s.t. VIII

حُلَفاء	حَلِيف	ally
بَواعِث	باعِث	motive
كَلِمات	كَلِمة	word
حَرَكات	حَرَكة	movement
جُمُوع	جَمْع	gathering/collection/horde
	قَبِيح	ugly/evil
مَوادّ	مادّة	material
آداب	أَدَب	literature/politeness
صَفَحات	صَفْحة	page
	سَواء	equality//equally
	حَوْلَ	around
	دُونَ	without/short of

1. هو see § 3:26.

2. مَفَرّ verbal abstract of I Type (ف ر ر), used as a synonym of بُدّ , see § 9:5.

5. أَرذال plural of رَذِيل

6. يجنى imperfect of I Type (ج ن ى).

12. تأهّبت feminine perfect of V Type (ء ه ب). لاح perfect of I Type (ل و ح).

13. 'Word' here and in ex. 18 below has an idiomatic sense of 'loyalty' (based on the idea of 'pledging one's word').

15. يؤول imperfect I Type (ء و ل).

17. تعطّل feminine imperfect II Type.

19. انسابت see note to section 11, ex. 3.

23. اضمحلّت see note to section 3, ex. 62.

25. جزاء verbal abstract I Type (ج ز ي).

29. أعدّ is here the imperfect of the verb of vague application of I Type, although indistinguishable in pattern (see § 8:2 last sentence) from that of the IV Type verb.

30. يوفّق imperfect of II Type (و ف ق) of vague application meaning 'have success granted to one', contrasting with the verb of specific application which means 'grant success (ه) to s.o.'.

13

تحمّس	يتحمّس	تحمُّس	be enthusiastic/fanatical V
رفض	يرفض	رفْض	reject/refuse (ه/ه) s.o./ s.t. I
قرأ	يقرأ	قراءة	read (ه) s.t. I
هاجر	يهاجر	مهاجرة	emigrate III
شقّ	يشقّ	شقّ	split (ه) s.t. I
استقبل	يستقبل	استقبال	meet/receive (ه) s.o. X

خافَ يَخاف خَوْف/مَخافة/خِيفة	fear (ه/ه) s.o./s.t. I
غَزا يَغْزُو غَزْو	raid/invade (ه/ه) s.o./s.t. I
نَصَرَ يَنْصُر نَصْر	help (ه) s.o. I
علّق يعلّق تعليق	comment (على) on s.t. II
جدّد يجدّد تجديد	renew (ه) s.t. II
أنشأ ينشئ إنشاء	raise/erect (ه/ه) s.o./s.t. IV
مَكَثَ يَمْكُث مُكوث	delay/tarry I
نَزَلَ يَنْزِل نُزُول	come down (ه/ه) to s.o./s.t. I

واجِب واجِبات	duty
أداء	payment/discharge
داعِي/داعٍ دَواعِي/دَواعٍ	reason/motive
عاصِمة عَواصِم	capital city
مُوَظَّف موظفون	official/employee
جَرِيدة جَرائِد	newspaper/journal
سِرّ أَسْرار	secret
مَذْهَب مَذاهِب	method/way/sect
مَنْهَج مَناهِج	procedure
كامِل	complete

إِخْوان / إِخْوة	أَخ	brother
آباء	أَب	father
أَيْدِي / أَيْدٍ	يَد	hand (feminine)
مَحَلّات	مَحَلّة	stopping place/quarter
أَسابِيع	أُسْبُوع	week
زُعَماء	زَعِيم	leader/spokesman

3. See § 6:2, § 6:3(iii).

5. Since 'delegates' in this sentence has not the form appropriate to an agent, it must be a direct object, and the agent must be the pronoun implied in the verb.

6. Since 'delegates' here has the agent form, and there is no direct object mentioned as is to be expected after a verb of this nature, the verb must be interpreted as a form of vague application and 'delegates' as a surrogate agent.

7. The case in this sentence is similar to that of the preceding example; for منح ordinarily requires two direct objects, one of the person and one of the thing, and since only the 'thing' object occurs in the sentence, 'Moriscos' must be taken as a surrogate agent and the verb as one of vague application.

8. Cp. ex. 3 above.

14. خوارج is an anomalous plural, the corresponding singular in usage being خارجيّ ; since it has the vowel pattern a - ā - i it belong to the class mentioned in § 13:10, which do not admit the terminal -n referred to in § 13:11, and hence it has no final alif marking its نصب status, such as is found with إثمًا in the following example.

17. See § 5:8.

18. تلقّاها perfect of V Type (ل ق ى) with object pronoun.

22. See § 10:11 and § 10:4.

23. سرًا is functionally an internal object representing a qualification of the omitted abstract of the verb (§ 13:17).

24. The internal objects here represent modifications and specifications of the concept which might have been expressed by the verbal abstract of the verb.

25. See § 4:9.

26. أذعن perfect IV Type.

29. إغارة verbal abstract of IV Type (غ و ر).

34. The first four Caliphs of Islam after the Prophet, before the division in Islam occasioned by the controversy over the assumption of the Caliphate by the Umayyad line, are

commonly known as الراشدون 'those who are on the right path', or by European Orientalists as 'Orthodox' or 'Rightly-guided'.

35. There are two 'circumstance' members of the sentence, the first expressed in phrase form as described in § 13:19(b), the second in clause form, § 11:1-2.

37. تُسْفِر feminine imperfect IV Type.

40. مُحاذٍ participle pattern of III Type verb (ح ذ و) in the undefined جرّ form; the defined counterpart would be المحاذي (§ 13:12).

46. أسابيع is devoid of terminal alif in accordance with § 13:10(b).

52. خَطَرًا here has the sense of 'significance' and is a qualifier of the intensified adjective. See Appendix (3) in Written Arabic for the abbreviation.

14

اعتزم يعتزم اعتزام resolve (على) on s.t. VIII

جَعَلَ يَجْعَل جَعْل make/do (ه) s.t. I

آثر يؤثر إيثار prefer (ه) s.t. (على) to s.t. IV [§ 3:12(iv)]

حَجَّ يَحُجّ حَجّ	go on pilgrimage I
جازَ يَجُوز جَواز	pass//be permissible I
أنقذ ينقذ إنقاذ	save (ه) s.o. IV
فَنَى يَفْنِي فَناء	perish/become extinct I
بَعَثَ يَبْعَث بَعْث	send (ب) s.o. I
أَحاط يُحيط إحاطة (٢وط)	surround (ب) s.o./s.t. IV
تمكّن يتمكّن تمكُّن	be enabled (من) to do s.t. V
أَعْطَى يُعْطِي إعطاء (عطو)	give (ه) s.o. (ه) s.t. IV
خَفَى يَخْفِي خفاء	conceal (ه) s.t. (على) from s.o. I
عَيَّنَ يعيّن تعيين	appoint (ه) s.o./determine (ه) s.t. II
اسْتَغْنَى يستغنِي استغناء	dispense (عن) with s.t. X

	مَسِيح	Christ/Messiah
مَيادِين	مَيْدان	field
	مُؤَقَّت	temporary
	نَفَر	small number of persons
	الآن	now
نُقَط/نِقاط	نُقْطة	important point
دَوائِر	دائِرة	circle/sphere

2. أَشْلَاء plural of شِلْو

3. مَجَانِيق Arabicized plural of مَنْجَنِيق, a word borrowed from Greek. سِهَام plural of سَهْم

7. رَأَى when followed by a verbal abstract or by a noun clause introduced by أَنْ, normally means 'see fit to do s.t.'.

10. يُؤْذُوا imperfect IV Type (ء ذ ى).

14. يُنْجِ imperfect جَزْم IV Type (ن ج و). مُتَنَصِّرُون participle of V Type.

15. يَبِدْ imperfect جَزْم I Type (ب ي د).

16, 17. The verb in each example is a جَزْم of X Type from root ج و ب . نَدًا verbal abstract I Type (ن د و).

19. يَعُدْ here is جَزْم of عَادَ (§ 9:7); other common roots which this unvowelled form could in other contexts represent are ع د د — ع د و — و ع د .

20. يَطْمَئِنُّوا imperfect from a four consonant root ط م ء ن

21. تَعْنَ imperfect جَزْم I Type (ع ن ى) in the form of vague application, which has the same sense as the VIII Type from the same root (vocabulary 4).

22. مُرّ vocabulary 1.

24. ذَكاء verbal abstract I Type (ذ ك ي). يُنمي imperfect IV Type. يُلَبِّ imperfect (جزم) II Type (ل ب ي).

15

قَصُرَ يَقْصُرُ قُصور	be short I
ضاقَ يَضيق ضِيق	be narrow/inadequate I
قَدِمَ يَقْدَم قُدوم/مَقْدَم	come (ه/هـ) to s.o./s.t. I
تَلا يَتْلو تِلْو	follow (ه/هـ) s.o./s.t. I
وَلِيَ يَلي وِلاية	govern (هـ) s.t. I
رَبّى يُرَبّي تَرْبية	rear/educate (ه) s.o. II
اِتَّخَذَ يَتَّخِذ اِتِّخاذ (ء خ ذ)	take (ه/هـ) s.o./s.t. VIII (§ 3:13, iii).
أَكَّدَ يُؤَكِّد تَأْكيد	emphasize/make certain (هـ) s.t. II
وَثِقَ يَثِق وُثوق	have confidence (بـ) in s.o./s.t. I
تَغَيَّرَ يَتَغَيَّر تَغَيُّر	undergo a change V

	مُدَّة	period
أَقْلام	قَلَم	pen
	تامّ	complete
	شَرْع	law/legal code
(ث ن و)	ثانی / ثانٍ	second (§ 13:12)
عادات/عَوائِد	عادة	custom/habit
	خِيانة	treachery
	زُهاء	about/approximately
مَظاهِر	مَظْهَر	manifestation
	شَفَوِيّ	oral

3. دِيار is formally a plural of دار , but has the specialized sense of 'country/region'.

4. إِلغاء verbal abstract IV Type (ل غ و).

11. مباشَرة verbal abstract III Type, functioning as internal object of the verb قَصدت .

13. أَزْياء plural of زِيّ (ز ی ی). تقاليد see note to section 9, ex. 8.

15. مخالفين participle III Type.

22. استطالت feminine perfect X Type (ط و ل).

27. دائم participle of فاعِل pattern (§ 8:8) of دام يدوم .

تنافي verbal abstract VI Type.

29. فُلُول plural of فَلّ . أغاروا see note to section 13, ex. 29.

31. تَجَرُّبِه verbal abstract V Type (ج ر ب), see § 13:12, with pronoun representing the theme of the verbal idea, § 15:2. إيّانا see § 15:7. بِلا see § 9:14, last sentence.

16

حِفْظ	يَحْفَظ	حَفِظَ	keep/remember (ه) s.t. I
التقاء (ل ق ى)	يلتقِي	التقَى	meet VIII
معاونة	يعاوِن	عاوَن	assist (ه) s.o. (على) to s.t. III
عَهْد	يَعْهَد	عَهِدَ	entrust (ب) s.t. (إلى) to s.o. I
سَمْع	يَسْمَع	سَمِعَ	hear (ه) s.t. I
تصوير	يصوِّر	صوَّر	depict (ه) s.t. II
نِتاج	يَنْتِج	نَتَجَ	result (من/عن) from s.t. I
	يَدْرِي	دَرَى	know (ه) s.t. I
وُجُود	يَجِد	وَجَدَ	find (ه/ه) s.o./s.t. I
حِسْبان	يَحْسَب	حَسَبَ	reckon/think I

أَحادِيث	حَدِيث	speech/narrative
	عَكْس	reverse

2. ألا the use of the negative attached to the query functional is idiomatic, and does not necessarily have the same connotation in Arabic as the corresponding English form 'Do you not think ... ?' but is frequently undifferentiated in sense from the simple query without negative.

3. شائقة participle فاعل pattern (ش و ق). ينوء imperfect I Type (ن و ء). يجهد here a form of vague application. كائناً has the نصب form occasioned by its use in a function parallel to that of a circumstance clause, § 13:19(b).

6. تُرى is here an idiomatic use, with a flavour of the colloquial style, in which ترى 'do you think?' is prefixed to or inserted into queries.

7. تسأل feminine imperfect II Type.

9. يدري this verb has the peculiarity that it is fairly common in the imperfect, but very rarely used in the perfect.

10. Cp section 5/6, ex. 46 and section 10, ex. 34.

11. خاطبني perfect of III Type with object pronoun. مائع see § 8:10.

14. مفتون participle مفعول pattern (ف ت ن). غرّك perfect of I Type (غ ر ر) with object pronoun.

17

agree (ه) with s.o. III	وافق	يوافق	موافقة
be in charge (ه) of s.t. V	تولّى	يتولّى	تولٍّ
be independent (ب) in s.t. X	استقلّ	يستقلّ	استقلال
begin (with following imperfect) I	أخذ	يأخذ	
surround (ب) s.o./s.t. VIII	احتاط	يحتاط	احتياط (2وط)
be complete I	تمّ	يتمّ	تمام
undertake/support (ه) s.t. V	تعهّد	يتعهّد	تعهّد
rule (ه/ه) s.o./s.t./judge (على) s.t. I	حكم	يحكم	حكم
arrange (ه) s.t. II	رتّب	يرتّب	ترتيب
exercise authority V	تحكّم	يتحكّم	تحكّم
talk (عن/في) about s.t. V	تحدّث	يتحدّث	تحدّث
be strong//tighten (ه) s.t. I	شدّ	يشدّ	شدّ
make a mistake IV	أخطأ	يخطئ	
family	أسرة	أسر	
stage/scene	مسرح	مسارح	
noble	نبيل	نبلاء	
article	مقالة	مقالات	

صُحُف	صَحِيفَة	newspaper
	مَلَأ	Assembly
أَهْداف	هَدَف	aim/goal
	تِجارَة	trade
زَوايا	زاوِيَة	angle
	حَياة	life

1. It is worth remarking that, while noun clauses after بَعْدَ and قَبْلَ may be introduced by ما or أَنْ , but with a preference for the latter, such clauses after عند are only introduced by ما .

3. كافٍ participle of فاعِل pattern (ك ف و), § 13:12.

4. نكون could be read as the imperfect of كان employed as a true predicate (§ 7:1), but it is more probable that what is intended is the imperfect of vague application نُكَوِّن of the II Type verb كَوَّن 'create/form'.

6. يزول is here a true predicate (§ 7:5). Since أَنْ followed by the perfect constitutes a factual noun clause (§ 6:5), this clause functions as the entity term after لولا in the manner described in § 12:12.

7. مِحَنًا plural of مِحْنَة (م ح ن).

9. تِباعًا an abstract functioning as internal object to the

verb تغير . أضحت feminine perfect IV Type (ض ح ي), being one of the verbs described in § 7:5 and a synonym of أصبح .

18. سيطرة see section 3, ex. 4.

20. سيّرت feminine of II Type (س ي ر).

22. لفي see § 6:3(i), last sentence.

23. ينتمي imperfect VIII Type (ن م ي). بني annexed form of بنين , a plural of ابن alternative to أبناء

24. Cp section 12, ex. 6. أروع intensified adjective pattern to رائع , on which see note to section 10, ex. 11.

26. إقطاعات see note to section 7, ex. 9.

28. والخلاف قائم circumstance clause, § 11:1(iii) and § 11:3.

29. ظلّ see § 7:5. يغذيها imperfect II Type (غ ذ ي).

30. عرقلة four consonant root. تنمية verbal abstract II Type (ن م ي), see § 3:11(ii). قيصر Arabicized form of 'Caesar'. بني حمير see note to ex. 23 above.

31. محور noun from root (ح و ر).

32. آنست feminine perfect IV Type (ء ن س), § 3:12(iv). أرحب intensified pattern to رحب 'spacious'. تباينًا see § 13:19(c).

34. نتيجةً is a نصب denoting motivation, § 13:19(a) and § 15:3(ii).

35. تجاهُل verbal abstract VI Type.

36. مميّزات plural of participle pattern مُفَعِّل II Type (م ي ز).

37. The object pronoun of the verb تخطئون is omitted (see § 4:8), but would have had the function of an internal object (§ 13:17), thus أخطأ خطأً 'he made a mistake', ما أخطأه 'the mistake which he made' (§ 4:9).

18

ملاقاة يلاقي لاقى	meet/encounter (ه/هـ) s. o. / s. t. III
اشتكاء يشتكي اشتكى	complain (هـ) of s. t. VIII
مراسلة يراسل راسل	correspond (ه) with s. o. III
احتواء يحتوي احتوى (ح و ي)	contain/comprise (على) s. t. VIII

فُرُوق فَرِيق	party
ضُرُوب ضَرْب	sort/kind
فُرُوع فَرْع	branch
أَنْواع نَوْع	sort/kind
شُرَفاء شَرِيف	noble

وِلايات	وِلايَة	province/state
تُهَم	تُهْمَة	suspicion
	عِداء	enmity
(اثْنَتان)	اثْنان	two
(ثَلاث)	ثَلاثَة	three
(أَرْبَع)	أَرْبَعَة	four
(خَمْس)	خَمْسَة	five
(سِتّ)	سِتَّة	six
(سَبْع)	سَبْعَة	seven
	ثَمانِيَة	eight (feminine ثَمانٍ , § 13:12)
(تِسْع)	تِسْعَة	nine
(عَشْر)	عَشَرَة	ten
	عِشْرُون	twenty
	ثَلاثُون	thirty
مِئات	مِائَة	hundred

2. غدت see note to section 7, ex. 25.

8. في الغالب see Wehr under غ ل ب ; the structure resembles that described in § 15:6 where a prepositional phrase as predicate precedes a noun clause which is the logical theme, as in 'it is false for us to say this'.

9. وَلَّاهُمَا perfect of II Type (و ل ى) with object pronoun.

11. إِذَنْ see §S:27(ii).

17. جَزِيرَة although properly meaning 'island', is sometimes used in the sense of 'peninsula'.

18. See § 13:21.

TRANSLATION

1

1. A few years. 2. The common danger. 3. A practical idea. 4. Local conflicts. 5. A religious tendency. 6. Western Europe. 7. The victorious army. 8. The Islamic peoples. 9. A final battle. 10. Another battle. 11. A Christian victory. 12. The national hopes. 13. National independence. 14. Some external dangers. 15. Spanish society. 16. Many wars. 17. The crusading campaigns. 18. Some small independent states. 19. Social customs. 20. The ruling classes. 21. An important document. 22. The great world religions. 23. The religions of the world. 24. The generality of men. 25. Affairs of state. 26. Statesmen. 27. The army of Islam. 28. The principles of decency. 29. The walls of Constantinople. 30. The surrender of Granada. 31. The rulers of the Islamic lands. 32. The reform of the state of the country. 33. The recent history of the Arab countries. 34. The states of the free world. 35. The frequency of European wars. 36. The last ruler of Granada. 37. The rulers of the other cities. 38. The ancient caliphs of Andalusia. 39. The centre of the new government. 40. The new centre of government. 41. The rise of a single central government. 42. The causes of the caliphate's weakness. 43. The disintegration of the Islamic empire. 44. The existence of the Islamic empire. 45. The necessity of strengthening [of]* the eastern empire. 46. The groups of crusading knights. 47. The principle of individual freedom. 48. The strength of Spanish Christendom. 49. The strength of the Christian principalites. 50. The debacle of Andalusian civilization. 51. The shadow of the new regime. 52. The national history of Egypt. 53. The subjugation of the weak successor states. 54. Ma'mun's earlier step. 55. The interior of the Arabian peninsula. 56. The ancient kingdom of Granada. 57. The modern city of Granada. 58. The commander of the Egyptian army. 59. The conclusion of a new peace treaty. 60. [A state strong of military power] A militarily powerful state. 61. [A factor strong of effect] A highly effective factor. 62. The lavishly extravagant governor of Granada. 63. Some short-term measures. 64. The government's short-term measures. 65. [A young man little of experience] An inexperienced young man. 66. [Bitter of

grievance] Bitterly aggrieved. 67. The populace with its bitter grievances. 68. An ill-starred and short-lived state. 69. Some precedent causes. 70. An historical precedent. 71. The caliphate's earlier prestige. 72. The great man of the Tartars. 73. The great offices of state. 74. Great statesmen. 75. Some of the great Christian knights. 76. Every internal conflict. 77. All means of defence. 78. All varieties of freedom. 79. The resisting of every fresh onslaught. 80. In every city. 81. In all the cities of the country. 82. In the whole country. 83. All the caliph's commands. 84. Each year. 85. The whole year. 86. Sometimes. 87. At every time. 88. At any time at all. 89. In any city at all. 90. In some dangerous crises. 91. The surrender of some of Al-Qadir's fortresses. 92. One of the neighbouring foreign states.

2(a)

1. These kingdoms. 2. These Mamluks. 3. This victorious king. 4. That drastic tyranny. 5. The affairs of this new state. 6. Those violent enemies. 7. The truth of this matter. 8. The realization of this aim. 9. The losses of the Franks in that battle. 10. [The like of this time] A time like this. 11. [The likes of these decisive battles] Such decisive battles as these. 12. [In the course of that] Meanwhile. 13. In consequence of that. 14. Because of that. 15. In the course of that hard-fought battle. 16. That continuing conflict. 17. His real aims. 18. Their national independence. 19. Her national unity. 20. Their decisive step. 21. Its western shore. 22. The opposing of their aggression. 23. The factors of its decline. 24. The disappearance of his empire. 25. In the way of recovering its land. 26. In consequence of the aggression of these Frankish campaigns. 27. All this. 28. In spite of all that. 29. In spite of all their tyrannous deeds. 30. All the eastern states. 31. In this journey of his. 32. The result of these researches of mine. 33. In the course of those researches of ours. 34. That aggressive policy of theirs. 35. These peace negotiations. 36. The whole of Iran. 37. Those selfsame Franks. 38. This same locality. 39. All the Arabs. 40. All his deeds.

2(b)

41. It is a world history. 42. This is the last of the book's chapters. 43. This is the last chapter. 44. This last chapter is [much of information] highly informative. 45. All the other accounts are false. 46. Every other account is false. 47. The true account is in the book of another historian. 48. Those are the phases of the Andalusian tragedy. 49. That is the origin of the decline of their empire. 50. It is the spirit of the Crusades. 51. The emir of Valencia was the husband of the sultan's daughter. 52. Bathing is necessary for health in a hot climate. 53. These social opinions are prevalent among them. 54. The social opinions prevalent among them are well-known. 55. [The need is extreme for the renewal of our view on this] We urgently need to reconsider this. 56. Our urgent need of reconsidering this is well-known. 57. [We are in need of reconsidering it] We need to reconsider it. 58. This is in spite of all their researches. 59. This has a connection with religion. 60. This city has religious prestige. 61. About the genuineness of this account there are a number of doubts. 62. They have an important role in the history of this country. 63. There is a danger to the state in the existence of these people. 64. This series of disasters had severe effects on the state. 65. This telegram had a great repercussion in Egypt. 66. This campaign was obliged to retrace the course of the Crusades from the beginning. 67. An army commander is obliged to realise his strategic aim by any means at all.

3

1. The king ordered the fortification of Mansura. 2. Christendom felt the overwhelming nature of the danger. 3. These efforts all failed. 4. He sent instructions to the Egyptian fleet for going out into the Palestinian waters; it went out under the command of Husam al-Din Lu'lu'; it gained control over those waters; it barred the way of approach to the coast for all the Frankish ships. 5. Their forces on the Nile approached Mansura. 6. The Christians employed a new weapon. 7. This important weapon played a great role in the Crusading wars. 8. The enemies of the sultan were victorious in that battle. 9. He won the victory over the government troops in some battles. 10. [They surprised the Franks with attacking] They

made a surprise attack on the Franks. 11. I met my friends there. 12. The forces of the sultan effected a junction with the Egyptian forces. 13. He himself participated in the battles. 14. The losses of the Franks have been estimated by western sources at some thousands. 15. Some of the princes assisted them in that. 16. The volcano of revolt erupted. 17. This corresponds to the prevailing cultural situation. 18. The book of 'the Conquests of the Countries' expresses the historic role of the Arabs. 19. This idea is centred on the city. 20. This book deals with the story of the Arabs of the south. 21. They were preparing to march south. 22. They have been speaking Arabic since the cradle. 23. The women were going into the city. 24. We shall explain this in the section [special to] devoted to * Egypt. 25. Some degree of doubt about this may well enter our minds. 26. The Muslim account perhaps exaggerates in estimating the losses of the Franks in that battle. 27. The Holy Land returned to the sovreignty of Islam. 28. Islam produced the idea of the nation. 29. The crusading idea [stands] is founded * on the conflict between Islam and Christendom. 30. The Franks [spent] made * a tremendous effort [for the setting up of] to throw * a bridge over the lake of Ushmun. 31. He erected a tower beside the city. 32. He was thereafter resident in the city until his death. 33. The sultan threw them in prison. 34. I for my part rested content with this situation. 35. This fresh Islamic eruption aroused the alarm of Christendom. 36. A great battle took place at 'Ain al-Jalut. 37. Saladin spent a few years in clearing up the affairs of the caliphate. 38. He published a proclamation of general amnesty. 39. The revolt collapsed. 40. They surrounded them on every side. 41. The peoples of the north escaped from the danger of extinction. 42. They gained control of Damietta. 43. The court replied to this in the affirmative. 44. These actions were viewed by the sultan as treachery. 45. [The malady grew severe in him] His malady grew worse. 46. The princes retired to their castles on the coast. 47. The sultan retired with his forces to Mansura. 48. This may well be true. 49. Revolt was general throughout all quarters of the kingdom. 50. This interest continued after the appearance of Islam. 51. The sultan's wife inspired the sick king with her own strength. 52. Conditions in the country were confused after his death. 53. Confusion ensued in their ranks. 54. Battles flared up in every quarter. 55. This is connected with the general trend of thought among

them. 56. The interest of the pre-Islamic Arabs in genealogies is connected with the social views prevalent among them.
57. The sultan's wife came to an agreement with [the men of the entourage] the courtiers * for the carrying on of business.
58. After that, the government troops turned northwards.
59. Christian Spain took its decisive step vis-à-vis Islam.
60. History shows us [much of the likes of that] many similar instances. 61. May God bring that to pass! 62. After that, his hopes faded. 63. The crookedness of his thought was apparent in his actions.

4(a)

1. The Goths whom Tariq ibn Ziyad crushed at the battle of Shadhuna. 2. The perilousness of the policy which Spain followed. 3. The historical views which they wished to express.
4. That uninterrupted warfare which Christian Spain waged on Muslim Spain. 5. That organized progress which Christendom achieved in the way of recovery of its lands. 7. The skill which Christian Spain displayed in profiting by the disintegration of the Islamic empire.

4(b)

8. The seclusion of women is a matter which is associated with the principles of decency. 9. It is a principle with the observance of which the Islamic state was concerned.
10. A civil disturbance which occurred in Damascus deflected them from their purpose. 11. He carried into effect an idea which had been revolving in his mind for a long time past, which was, the expulsion of every Muslim. 12. He fitted out a large army with which he moved into the country of the Armenians. 13. This historical school arose from roots which differ from [the roots] those* of the Medina school. 14. Islam was being set aflame by a new force, which was the Seljuk state. 15. Louis sent his messengers to the king of Egypt with a letter in which he warned him of the necessity of surrender.
16. The history of Andalusia often presents us with the story of a Muslim emir who fell into [the captivity of] the hands of * the Christians. 17. They are working for a single aim, which is the defence of Islam. 18. This is a phenomenon which attracts attention. 19. There are factors which have led to the

growth of these tendencies. 20. The persistence of this situation is leading to an internal revolution which will [be general throughout the country] involve the whole country. 21. The universal crisis through which the west is passing has a manifest effect on historical studies. 22. I have here turned to the factors which led to the rise of the science of history among the Arabs. 23. The motives which set alight the flame of strife in Spain are themselves the ones which directed the idea of the Crusades towards the east. 24. They lacked that enthusiasm which is the spirit of the crusading campaigns. 25. They penetrated the Muslim kingdom of Rum which the Seljuk Turks had established. 26. They wished to smash that power which had ruined their plans. 27. They are the people who believe in a Creator. 28. At the moment at which the volcano of revolution erupted, Spain took advantage of the elements of confusion which were prevalent among the Islamic kingdoms. 29. The motives which have led to historical writing among the Arabs are connected with cultural developments. 30. This became plain from the policy of repression which the founder of new Spain had prescribed. 31. Ferdinand concluded all the treaties which would guarantee security for them. 32. The Islamic explosion in the east aroused the fears of the Byzantine empire which was the bastion of Christianity on the east. 33. Butrus Pasha is the person who signed the Sudan agreement in 1899. 34. He granted him what he asked. 35. He did with them [the like of what their predecessors did] much the same as their predecessors had done. 36. That which befell the people of Baghdad will befall them also. 37. We have, in the reign of Mansur, something which makes this plain. 38. Charlemagne threw Islam back to [that which is beyond] the other side of * the Pyrenees. 39. They succeeded in the thing for which they were striving. 40. The mind of every person who has known something [of which the name is] called * freedom comprehends this principle. 41. This is the position of a person who claims his rights. 42. He appeared before men in the guise of someone who wishes to brandish the constitutional idea. 43. Some of those who had been exhausted by the struggle inclined towards making peace. 44. The ruling classes, in spite of the urge of roaming which possessed them, were bound by numerous ties to their national homelands. 45. This is in the light of the critical examination which we have taken upon [our shoulder] ourselves. 46. They gained control, without resistance, of the stores of food which were in Damietta. 47. He directed some attention to Mecca because of the religious prestige which it had. 48. They killed the Christian menfolk who were in the city; they took prisoner those of their womenfolk who were there. 49. I asked him [about the amount of contentment of the Wafd] how far the Wafd was contented * with [what in the way of luck in success his effort had had] the degree of success which had attended his effort. 50. Ruin has come swiftly upon whatever country they gained control of. 51. They opposed whatever measure we embarked on.

5/6

1. The abandonment of national costume is a difficult matter. 2. War is either for the spreading of the cause of religion or for the crushing of enemies. 3. A new danger, however, assailed the country. 4. There is a happy augury in the Arab revival which we behold among the ranks of the Arab peoples. 5. His policy aims at weakening, or indeed destroying, the authority of the Khedive. 6. History shows us how this tyrannical policy wronged the greatness of Spain. 7. The Franks learned from some of their spies - or from traitors - of the existence of some fords in the lake of Ushmun, and by these they crossed to its western shore. 8. This is what took place in Egypt; in Syria, the governor of Aleppo set about fitting out an army. 9. This policy [there is lacking for it argument] is indefensible. 10. So far as Ya'qubi is concerned, he wrote a general history. 11. As for Damascus, Hulagu's lieutenant assured its populace of immunity. 12. The murder was motivated by fanaticism. 13. Any prime minister, however, is concerned about the dignity of [rule] office. 14. Perhaps there are therein some indications of the correctness of their opinion. 15. Perhaps what occurred afterwards may explain the reaction which was taking place. 16. He resolved on suing for peace in the hope that he might perhaps escape the wrath of the Tartars. 17. The decision obliged the Muslim to submit to embracing Christianity or else to abandon his homeland. 18. His way to the realization of this objective was that he should restore to the Islamic east its unity. 19. He was able to cut the armies of the Christian principalities to pieces. 20. He is reluctant to conclude treaties. 21. Christian Spain was able to take advantage of the elements of disturbance. 22. We urgently need to understand the new theories and trends

in the science of history. 23. This blow is guaranteed to destroy every plan and preparation for meeting the enemy. 24. The negotiation ended in agreement on the release of Louis and his companions, and that the Franks should surrender Damietta. 25. The majority, however, refused to listen to any fresh promises; that was because the Arabs had become convinced that Christian Spain was [devoid of trustworthiness] utterly faithless. 26. They surrendered Granada after they had exhausted all means of defence. 27. The emirs concealed the news of his death until they arrived at Damascus. 28. He then moved to Armenia, and conquered it anew, after the Armenians had broken their treaty. 29. This ministry was specially characterized by the fact that it included [elements of the youth] younger elements. 30. He knew that his troops would desert him. 31. I learned, when I got back from Mansura, that they had made an effort to put this idea into practice. 32. I mentioned that the motive for the muder was perhaps some political belief which had established itself in the mind of the murderer. 33. The truth is that these Mamluks had been exploiting their authority. 34. [The manifest thing is] It is evident* that they learned of the sultan's death from some of their spies, and felt that the opportunity was favourable for [letting fall] striking * their blow. 35. They sense that they have an important historical role. 36. In that year the news reached him that the Tartars had raided northern Syria. 37. That is because Louis is being urged on by a religious tendency. 38. This is in addition to the fact that local interests [great harm befell them] were greatly damaged* by the government's proceedings. 39. The Pope permitted him to wage war in the name of religion, provided that he would rule the land, after the conquest, in the name of the Papacy. 40. We can, nevertheless, describe Charles V's attitude in relation to the Arabs [by moderation in comparison with the attitude] as relatively moderate in comparison with that * of his son Philip. 41. This is the only way out, unless England resorts to armed force. 42. It was impossible for this situation to continue, unless these people were intending that it should lead to revolt. 43. [He is possessed of some part of goodness of administration] He is, to some extent, a good administrator, * nevertheless the whole population of the city hates him. 44. The enlightened class, however, saw these reforms to be essential. 45. We can consider the battle of Hattin to be characterized by an outstanding importance;

that is because it paved the way for the recovery of Jerusalem. 46. In that case, they regarded these decisions as binding. 47. In spite of these difficulties, we feel that it is possible for us to study the history of the Arabs.

7

1. This was the feeling of the English leaders. 2. The Jews were the victims of the policy of repression. 3. Mustafa 'Abdarraziq was the person who succeeded in this business. 4. It is necessary that Egypt's attitude in this war should be that of neutrality. 5. Fate willed that this great hero should be the conqueror of the Latin kingdom. 6. The council of state was watching for an opportunity. 7. They used to despatch the Frankish prisoners to Cairo. 8. That is because Louis was being urged on by a religious tendency. 9. The Seljuk Turks had taken possession of the greatest part of the bases in Syria. 10. At the time of the collapse of the caliphate [Toledo, its magistrate had assumed command in it] the magistrate of Toledo had assumed command there. 11. He had the victory. 12. The intrigues of the Turks had a great influence on this disintegration. 13. His propaganda had great effect in arousing the nation's enthusiasm. 14. This campaign was obliged to retrace the course of the crusading wars from their beginning. 15. Earlier ages may well have their far-reaching effect on present developments. 16. This has no connection with religion. 17. Egypt has no advantage to gain by means of this war. 18. There is no danger to the state in their existence. 19. [I am not a believer] I do not believe * that this victorious king can have had [of gallantry and nobility what he had of goodness of luck] so much gallantry and nobility as mere good luck. 20. I therefore feel that I owe France a debt which I shall never forget, unless I prove ungrateful; and it is not in my nature to be ungrateful. 21. We do not need to pass judgment on these wars. 22. These atrocities continued to befall the unfortunate people. 23. These Mamluks [began to be masters] gained the mastery * of the fortresses. 25. This state became strong and powerful, and began to rival the Islamic state. 26. The holy lands were once more under Islamic sovereignty.

8

1. Any opponent was cast into the fires of the Inquisition.
2. Their demands were presented to the court. 3. They were expelled under safe-conduct to Fez with their families.
4. Some efforts for negotiation were made. 5. Christian Spain was routed at Zallaqa. 6. The sultan hurried to the fortress which had been erected in the neighbourhood of the camp.
7. [The country was afflicted afresh] Fresh afflictions befell the country. 8. These decisions were considered to be binding.
9. He may perhaps be censured for some amount of severity.
10. He was taken by surprise by the arrival of Sheikh Ahmad and was compelled to make his submission to him. 11. During the time of the caliph Mustansir Billah, many of the offices of state were entrusted to the Jews. 12. This is a phenomenon which may sometimes be seen. 13. They were, however, subsequently routed and compelled to evacuate Damietta.
14. Many examples of this phenomenon may be found in history.
15. The prince sought safe-conduct from them and was granted what he asked. 16. In all these battles [slain men and captives were lost] there were losses by death and capture.
17. Ma'mun got in touch with a man called Al-Hakam ibn 'Ukasha. 18. Nasim Pasha's ministry resigned and 'Adli Pasha was called on to form the ministry. 19. He took refuge in the village of Minya which lies on the Nile. 20. The Franks made a tremendous effort to resist. 21. Something expressive of the aims of the church is to be found in his policy. 22. He demanded that an official funeral should be held for Sir Lee Stack, and it was duly held. 23. The British government demanded that the government of the Sudan should be permitted to increase the area of cotton cultivation. 24. 'Adli Pasha remembered his previous ministry, and the disturbances and demonstrations which had then occurred, in which [bloods had flowed and lives had been destroyed and properties had been pillaged] there had been bloodshed, loss of lives and pillage of property. 25. The idea expressed in this section demonstrates the correctness of our view. 26. The idea here indicated may well convince us of that truth. 27. Any agreed policy ought to be carried out. 28. They set on foot propaganda in the name of the caliph who it was alleged had escaped.
29. They sought for a sheikh of acknowledged experience.
30. Any minister whose conduct is suspect of such a tendency may well be forced to retire.

9

1. The government did not proceed further than that. 2. They did not cease speaking Arabic. 3. We may well be unable to follow these speculations. 4. We do not mean thereby that Christian Spain was unacquainted with causes of internal dissension. 5. Allenby still continued to be the British High Commissioner in Egypt. 6. The prince soon dismissed him from office. 7. That did not, however, prevent the ministry from proceeding to carry out the programme which [its chief] the prime minister * had laid down. 8. A remnant of ancient traditions continued to link this people with its past. 9. [It is necessary for a man that he should make long the searching] A man must search long * for the truth, and not rest content with that much of it which he thinks he has reached. 10. They embarked on [a series to which there is no end] an unending series * of wars. 11. There is no dispute about the heroism of this great fighter. 12. The prince has no power at all. 13. Sidqi Pasha felt that he must inevitably combat this campaign with all his strength. 14. He has no course but to flee the country. 15. We may, after all this effort, achieve only general outlines. 16. He has only the name of sultan. 17. His life lasted thereafter only a short space of time. 18. Iraq is hardly ever free from these epidemics every year. 19. It was no longer in his mind to pursue the matter. 20. They were marching [to the conquest of] to subdue * some outlying bases which hardly had the strength to repel a powerful enemy. 21. They were certain that Christian Spain had no sense of honourable obligation, and that she was unfit to be trusted. 22. There was in the committee no small nu mber of members of the government. 23. This is something different from the author's meaning. 24. Without a study of these aspects, it will be impossible for us to criticize the researches of other people. 25. The Islamic idea filled his mind, and he believed in nothing else. 27. This has several meanings. 28. Several sources have said this. 29. The battles which occurred thereafter were merely a final phase. 30. He cannot be criticized for any severity, apart from his violence in the war against Syria. 31. [There was not in his policy except something expressive] His policy was simply expressive * of the aims of the church. 32. Ferdinand, however, was not in the least reluctant to conclude treaties. 33. As for the effects of the Crusades, space does not suffice for dealing with them; we can,

however, say that they were the mainspring of European nationalism. 34. [Half of a century and not anything else] A mere half century * separates us from that age. 35. There were among them some persons who had no connection with constitutional expertise. 36. Wars continued without intermission to the time of his death. 37. The non-arrival of the expected reinforcements had a far-reaching effect on the prince's spirit. 38. He based his opposition on his inability to cooperate with Sidqi Pasha. 39. Everyone was expecting that the non-acceptance of his demand would lead to his immediate resignation from the ministry. 40. It is believed that he will certainly be unable to form the ministry. 41. He declared that he would on no account return to Egypt without the result which had been agreed on. 42. He announced that he would repress them [without pity] pitilessly.

10

1. They overran the country in less than a century. 2. The government did something worse and more harmful than that. 3. The conflict of Islam and Christendom has perhaps never witnessed, since the battle of Zallaqa, any conflict greater in its events and consequences than the decisive battle of Mansura. 4. The religious conflagration in the west was weaker than in the east. 5. He is the greatest of the knights of Granada. 6. He is among the greatest heroes of Islam. 7. This campaign was the greatest of the Crusades. 8. He related the horridest stories of the Seljuks' tyranny. 9. Among the most beautiful of these monuments is the Zahiriyya library. 10. He took by storm the best-defended of their fortresses, and the remotest of their frontier points. 11. They uttered threats of the most terrible kinds of damage. 12. This was the greatest factor in the dissolution of his empire. 13. This deed was the greatest error and crime. 14. This campaign was in fact the best entitled of the Crusades [to this description] to be so described. 15. We are in most urgent need of the study of history. 16. He raided the remotest and best-defended of their northern strongholds. 17. The Jews were the first victims of the policy of repression. 18. Granada was the last stronghold of Islam. 19. He accomplished a great work for the good of the country. 20. They gained control of the last Islamic stronghold. 21. The first crusading conflict did not

take place in the plains of Syria. 22. Therefore, the first condition which the king of the Mongols stipulated was the prevention of these people from settling in the land of Egypt. 23. As for the mass of the nation, they were in the most terrible condition [from] of * poverty and hunger. 24. She was the first, as she was also the last, queen of Islamic Egypt. 25. The sultan was to the utmost degree feeble. 26. He ordered the striking of coinage from the basest variety of brass. 27. Louis mobilized his great expedition. 28. He was buried under the dome of the great Zahiriyya madrasa. 29. The sultanate of Rum was in Asia Minor. 30. The series of great wars which are known by the name of Crusades began. 31. Toledo was among the best defended cities of the Middle Ages. 32. The knights and lords opposed the liberties of the middle classes and the populace. 33. Death is the best thing you will meet from them. 34. This was the most important thing with the investigation of which the courts were concerned. 35. The most ancient trace of Iranian nationalism [which has arrived] to make its appearance * comes in poetry. 36. The crusading idea [is wider in scope] has a wider scope * than those conflicts which the historian calls Crusades. 37. The armies of Egypt were the earliest of the Islamic armies in repelling the crusading onslaught and [were the most extreme of them in violence against it], and reacted against it the most vehemently. 38. Abdallah [was particularly much in intelligence and reflection] was preeminently intelligent and reflective.

11

1. They moved towards Tiberias, seeking for a place in which there was water. 2. Saladin had sent messages in all directions summoning men to war. 3. Islam poured out in the plains of France, threatening Christendom and the nations of the north. 4. Ma'mun kept watching for opportunities for putting his scheme into execution. 5. They returned to France after a few years [while ambassadors were accompanying them] accompanied by ambassadors * from the caliph. 6. The sultan's march seemed like a torrent, as it swept away those who stood in its path. 7. He came to Egypt with the intention of carrying out Cromer's policy. 8. The Franks retired towards a hillock at the nearby village of Hattin, in order to entrench themselves there. 9. [Before that by some months]

Some months previously*, he had gone to central France with the intention of visiting the châteaux of the Loire. 10. Deputations of the people of Damascus came out to him, to announce its submission. 11. He desired me to get in touch with the man, in order that I might ascertain from him what would happen. 12. I got to know him for the first time while I was travelling in Lebanon. 13. Death overtook him while he was on his way to Damascus. 14. They marched towards the village of Fariskur, while their ships were proceeding parallel to them on the Nile. 15. He greeted me [while a smile was on his face] with a smile on his face. 16. The caliph's ambassadors returned to Baghdad, having with them a collection of gifts and presents. 17. All the Frankish princes and knights were captured, in the forefront of them being the king of Jerusalem. 18. The siege continued, with the troops of Islam repelling the raiders from on top of the walls. 19. Muhammad ibn Umayya was victorious over the government troops, his fame became widespread, and the Arabs gave him their allegiance. At this point Don Juan marched with his great army to Guadix, then to the Baza area, with uninterrupted battles flaring up between him and the rebels in these regions. 20. The king of Egypt hurried [returning] back * from a campaign in Syria, although he was lying sick on his stretcher. 21. Thus does Condé, although he is a Spanish Christian, describe the court's decision. 22. They were not able to defend themselves, since they were unarmed. 23. Since the Arabic language alone had not now the power to unite the Arabs, there [was no escape from] had to be * some other basis on which Arab nationalism could rest.

12

1. If it becomes plain that the Allies wish to apply these principles, he on his part will adhere to them. 2. If the day comes on which there is no avoiding a divergence in our views, we shall consider the matter afresh. 3. The sultan swore that, if he could get hold of this treacherous prince, he would kill him with his own hand. 4. He warned them that, if the city did not obtain immunity, the Franks would kill their children and womenfolk. 5. Whenever affairs of state are in the hands of base men, you can expect speedy dissolution for this state. 6. If we bestow on Saladin any other description than

[the Islamic description] that of Muslim*, or if we attribute to him nationalistic or local motives, we shall thereby do wrong to the career of this great Islamic hero. 7. When Egypt becomes independent, there will be no harm in entering into an alliance with a strong nation like England. 8. [Whatever his statements may be in respect of truth or exaggeration] Whatever truth or exaggeration there may be in his statements, * his propaganda has had enormous effect. 9. They authorized the Wafd to strive for independence [wherever it might find a way to effort] by whatever means it could find. 10. He will guarantee men their rights so long as they [continue in possession of] retain * their religion. 11. We cannot make progress so long as we do not comprehend this principle.
12. Christendom made preparations to defend itself whenever the spectre of this danger appeared. 13. The northern principalities used to forget their dessensions and rally round the banner of religion whenever Islam threatened them from the south. 14. Had this been recognized, it would have led to a split in the country. 15. I asked myself, what would the situation have come to if England had not followed this path.
16. That would have been possible, had the war not occurred.
17. The nation's advantage from these studies would have been greater, if other events had not occurred and frustrated the march of the Egyptian movement towards its objectives.
18. It would have been in the power of these new Muslim states to erect a strong barrier [in the face of] against * Christian Spain, if only their loyalties had been united. 19. The hordes of Tartars poured into Syria, and had it not been for the fact that the Egyptian armies repulsed them at the battle of 'Ain al-Jalut, they would have carried away everything in their path. 20. England defended the Egyptian people in the war, and had it not been for her, the Turks would have entered Egypt. 21. He was on the verge of killing him, had not the caliph prevented him from doing so. 22. Had it not been for the fact that discord occurred among the Mongol princes themselves, Chuban would have persisted in his horrid deeds.
23. Had it not been for this success, his fame would have waned. 24. It is not possible to study Arab history without rewriting the historical source material; otherwise, history will be mingled with tales and literary pieces. 25. He obliged the Arabs to embrace Christianity, otherwise their reward would be death. 26. The Crusades are a page of the history of Egypt, although they are at the same time a page of the

general history of Islam. 27. He used to consult his own inspiration, although there was nothing in his policy except that which expressed the aims of the church. 28. We perceived this swift change in the attitude of the public, although we felt at the same time the controversy was growing more intense in the minds of others. 29. I used to be acquainted with him, although I was not reckoned among his friends. 30. He did not succeed in realizing his objective, although he was able to cut the armies of the Christian principalities to pieces. 31. Even if the allies leave him in the lurch, he does not consider that revolution will assure the country its independence. 32. Egypt's attitude in this war must be that of neutrality, no matter whether England participates in it or does not. 33. No matter whether the minister does or does not support it, it is my view.

13

1. The Muslims surrendered Granada to the victorious enemy. 2. The Egyptian troops [became enthusiastic and set to work their swords on the remnants of the Crusaders] with great fervour put the remnants of the Crusaders to the sword. 3. As regards the delegates, they have been rejected by the government. 4. The truth is that the historians are exaggerating this. 5. He authorized the delegates to negotiate. 6. The delegates were authorized to negotiate. 7. The Moriscos were granted one month for departure. 8. The affair was not followed up, for the delegates had been rejected by the government. 9. I felt that we owed a duty which it was imperative to fulfil for the homeland. 10. We do not believe that there is any doubt about this. 11. This bad example was a cause of the Muslims' despair. 12. The caliph continued to be resident in the capital. 13. If this demonstrates anything, it is that the ministers consider themselves to be officials. 14. The government considered them to be dangerous insurrectionaries. 15. The reading of 'As-Siyasa' was considered to be a crime against the Wafdists. 16. The Muslims of Andalusia emigrated to Africa. 17. Many of the thinkers and historians of the west have previously [judged according to this] formed this judgment. 18. He inflicted on him a blow with his sword, which the sultan received on his hand, and it was split open to the forearm. 19. He made a great slaughter of the Muslims.

20. They made a great massacre of the Muslims, in which the governor of Granada died. 21. The king [received the caliph's ambassadors with the finest reception] accorded the caliph's ambassadors the most friendly reception. 22. In this battle the Franks [were routed with an extreme rout and were cut to pieces with the worst of cutting] were utterly routed and most terribly cut to pieces. 23. They are conducting secret negotiations with the kings of Africa. 24. [He annihilated them with killing and capture] He killed them and took them prisoner, to the point of annihilation. 25. We are able to draw great profit from such procedures and methods as we discover preparatory to laying down historical methods proper to our own studies. 26. Some of them submitted out of anxiety over their homeland. 27. The Mamluks had razed the city walls for fear of the Franks' arrival there. 28. Many withdrew to Africa for fear of vengeance. 29. The Castilians had marched to Valencia with the [desire] intent * to make a raid on it. 30. Alexander the Macedonian conquered most of Asia and part of Africa carrying with him the Hellenistic culture of his own land. 31. They rushed [being enthusiastic] enthusiastically * to the aid of religion. 32. The earliest historical compositions have not reached us in a state of completeness. 33. The bands of Crusading knights poured into the east and swept victorious through the Muslim kingdom of Rum. 34. We observe the author of the book to state, when commenting on his death, 'It was a day [with the like of which Islam and the Muslims have never been afflicted since the Orthodox Caliphs were lost] of disaster for Islam and the Muslims unparallelled since the demise of the Orthodox Caliphs'. 35. Louis came to Egypt to renew the era of the Crusade, and accompanied by some of the Christian princes with their troops. 36. This king was a personality of great glamour. 37. This war did not yield any [results possessed of significance] significant results. 38. Their knights advanced under the command of the king of France's brother. 39. Antioch fell into the hands of the Crusaders. 40. He took refuge in a fortress lying opposite to the city. 41. [Controversy is occurring] There is a current controversy * on this subject. 42. He withdrew, carried on his stretcher, with his forces to Mansura, this being the place which his father had founded. 43. The crusading idea is earlier in time and broader in scope than those battles. 44. The soil of France is not [greater in fertility] more fertile * than the soil of Egypt. 45. He remained there for some days.

46. Local conflicts continued for some weeks. 47. The Crusaders lingered for a little while before the walls of Tripoli. 48. They came down into Egypt for the first time in the days of Al-Malik al-Kamil. 49. He was for a long time investigating this matter. 50. The rebels chose a new leader in place of him. 51. This state is adjacent on the south to the borders of Palestine. 52. The east [returned on him with a number of attacks] made a number of ripostes to him*, of which the one with the greatest significance was in the year 17 B.C.

14

1. They resolved to make out of their principalities one united front. 2. They preferred in the end to swallow up the dismembered Eastern Empire, rather than to go on pilgrimage to the tomb of Christ. 3. The Crusaders were able finally, after bombarding the city [with violence] heavily * with mangonels and arrows, to take the walls by storm and gain control of it. 4. They crossed into Andalusia in order to save it from the danger of extinction. 5. He sent his troops to conquer for him the castles and fortresses surrounding Tabriz. 6. Islam strove to preserve its land and its sovreignty. 7. The Crusaders had, since the fall of their kingdom in Jerusalem, thought fit to turn the field of conflict to Egypt, in order that they might crush that power. 8. The Muslims had appreciated that, in order that they might be enabled to put an end to the aggression of the west, it would be necessary that one thing should be achieved. 9. They were not able to follow up this victory, so as to take the city by a final assault. 10. They announced that they would by no means harm anyone. 11. The sources have given us no conclusive answer. 12. He had only a few years of life after that. 13. Not a century has passed since that time. 14. Those who turned Christian did not save themselves from persecution and oppression. 15. No pity was shown in carrying out the laws. 16. He did not respond to their appeal. 17. They did not respond to his appeal. 18. The Crusaders saw no severe campaign after that of Saladin. 19. The controversy was no longer confined to [the being of history] whether history is * science or literature. 20. The leaders of the church and the princes of the west did not, however, feel reassured at this temporary respite.

21. The east, on its part, did not gain anything from engaging in these battles with fanatical hordes who were only concerned with fire and the sword and with winning booty. 22. These harsh truths were not concealed from the Crusaders, and it was not unknown to them that they were marching to the conquest of scattered and mutually jealous bases and regions. 23. Religious enthusiasm in the west did not lead to great and far-flung conquests like those which the Islamic states undertook. 24. Gregory was unable, however, in spite of his cleverness, to inspire in the princes that enthusiasm which was the spirit of the crusades; therefore his propaganda did not bear fruit, and only a small number of people responded to it. 25. Let us now review the main points of this valuable book. 26. Let us take a definite subject as an example. 27. Let us leave the sphere of speculation and return to the narrative of events. 28. Let us dispense with pursuing this matter.

15

1. This may perhaps be too long to describe. 2. The period of his reign was too short for the development of this idea. 3. The Aleppo region, and Aleppo itself, [met] suffered * from the Mongols' atrocities [that for the mention of which the pen is too inadequate] experiences such as no pen can adequately describe. 4. They sought for an opportunity of abrogating the treaty. 5. The Crusaders, however, landed on the day following their arrival. 6. Fate willed that Philip should be the carrier out of this policy. 7. They saw in him the complete image of the statesman. 8. The fall of Antioch, after it had stood out against a siege which lasted several months, was a result of the treachery of some of the local leaders. 9. She is a legal wife of the sultan. 10. The Moriscos are enemies of Spain. 11. This campaign was aimed directly at Egypt, in order to make of her a battleground of the holy war and a prize of the church. 12. In the second year of his reign he thought about restoring the caliphate to its early status. 13. Costume, language, morals and social customs are all traditions of education and convention. 14. He took the city of Amid as his capital. 15. He banished those of them who were in opposition. 16. Large numbers of them emigrated to Fez. 17. A court of clerics was set up. 18. A continuous struggle on the part of Islam took place. 19. He regarded any

opposition by his friends as treachery. 20. The Crusades are in one sense a page of the national history of Egypt. 21. This was another phase of that general conflict. 22. The unintermitting battles which took place after that on the plains of Syria and Egypt between the Muslims and the Franks for about a century and a half were only another phase of that general conflict. 23. [The acceptance of his resignation with this speed] This speedy acceptance of his resignation * was perhaps a manifestation of anger. 24. The battle was in fact prelude to a new chapter of this war. 25. It is to be expected that the narratives should be oral. 26. It is certain that all the lands subject to Mongol rule were at that time under the control of Chuban. 27. One of the causes of this perpetual tension is the incompatibility of bedouin and civilized life. 28. The author of this book is not a person in whom we can place confidence. 29. A thing which is worthy of remark in this period is that the remnants of the Crusaders who were on some of the Syrian frontiers seized the opportunity of the Tartar onslaught and made raids on the country. 30. The motive of his composing this book is not obvious. 31. Our opposition to him and his defiance of us remained [without alteration] unchanged.

16

1. Do you believe that the Castilians will observe their treaties? 2. I said, 'Do you think that the meeting of 'Abdul'aziz Fahmi and Sa'd Zaghlul will be of assistance towards this?'. 3. Do you think the formation of a 'great' ministry, as the French call it, to be an easy matter in Egypt? It is a troublesome business [with which would be burdened anyone] which would be a burden to anyone * who is entrusted with the formation of the ministry, [he being] be he * who he may. 4. Do we need to say that the struggle between Islam and Christianity has not ceased? 5. Will then the armed forces of Egypt march beside the Turkish forces, or will they [stand upon] adopt an attitude of * neutrality? 6. I afterwards asked myself, however, 'Supposing the speech [its basis had not been] had not been based on * the fact that he did not form the ministry, and had it been he on the contrary who was to form it, would I have heard from him what I did? Or is it the case that this speech was a reflection of his true personality?'. 7. If the Ottoman troops wish to pass through the territory of

Egypt, what will her attitude be? Will she facilitate transit for the Turkish troops? 8. From what does this antagonism arise? 9. He hardly knows why he was summoned. 10. The most important thing with the investigation of which the courts were concerned was whether the decision should be considered binding. 11. He addressed an enquiry to me, as to whether I would find anything that would prevent me from meeting the minister, and I replied that nothing would prevent me from doing so. 12. Think about this principle, and you will feel sure of its soundness. 13. With what excitement that stirred our minds! 14. They said to him, 'Deluded youth! [a position has misled you] you have been misled by a position * in which you imagine yourself to be master of the situation'.

17

1. My uncle was, at the time of my arrival from Europe, residing in Alexandria. 2. Is it not then possible by some means or other to override the opinion of the British Foreign Office? 3. They were reluctant to agree until they could obtain an adequate guarantee. 4. The policy of England aimed in the first place at the establishment of the first Wafd ministry, until the constitutional ministry should come into existence which would be able to negotiate. 5. His family continued to hold power in the principality of Hira until the Muslim Arabs subjugated it. 6. They resolved to revolt against Chuban, and civil war broke out, so that Mongol rule was on the verge of perishing, had it not been for the fact that he showed great cleverness. 7. The city of Basra met with severe trials from them, to the extent that it was said that they seized from its inhabitants more than half their wealth. 8. He had independant control of Mecca until his brother took it from him. 9. The Latin state began making repeated raids on the territories and bases around it until it became a power [which had its significance] to be reckoned with. 10. Only a few years had passed [upon] since * the surrender of Granada when the Spaniards began to modify the treaty. 11. Hardly had they moved into the new regime, however, when they were ordered to leave the country. 12. The court's decision had not yet been promulgated when disturbances broke out in every quarter. 13. Hardly had he finished speaking when the knight drew near. 14. Before dawn had broken they

surrounded the Franks. 15. Only a short time had elapsed since the defeat of Abraha when a fresh popular national movement arose in the realm of Himyar for freeing the country from the domination of the Abyssinians. 16. The scene of this conflict was, until the following century, in Europe. 17. Musa ibn Nusayr pursued them as far as the foothills of the Pyrenees. 18. By the control of Beirut, control was assured to him of the whole Syrian coast from Alexandretta as far as Alexandria. 19. When they reached Constantinople, they undertook to govern it in the name of the emperor. 20. When the Crusaders marched against Syria, Egypt seized the opportunity and despatched her troops to Jerusalem. 21. When Baybars had arranged his internal and external affairs, he resolved to fight against the Crusaders who were still in control of some areas of Palestine. 22. I was at home one day, when my uncle came to me. 23. This Castilian name concealed an ancient Arab lineage, since its bearer was affiliated to the [sons of Umayya] Umayyads. 24. Thereby we do wrong to the career of the hero, since we strip him of the most attractive of the [garments] attributes * of his heroism. 25. The study of this subject is, however, difficult, since the earlier historical compositions have not reached us. 26. All classes among the Christians profited from every territory wrested from Muslim Spain, because the nobles gained new fiefs, and the middle classes hurried into the new cities. 27. All of a sudden, there was Lutfi Pasha [informing men] bombarding the public * with articles in the press. 28. Did not 'Adli Pasha go in 1921 to negotiate with England, at a time when [dispute was standing] there was an open dispute * between him and Sa'd Pasha, and straight away this dispute was seized upon as an excuse on the part of the British Foreign Minister [in order that he might be extreme in] for intensifying * his demands? 29. Thereby the idea began to gain strength, and Muhammad Mahmud Pasha continued to support and nourish it [by his means] by all means in his power * until, when it was ripe and everyone had agreed to it, and the press had [talked on the matter of it] discussed it *, nothing remained but that it should be announced to the Assembly in an official manner which would [place the existing government before the fait accompli consisting in it] face the existing government with a fait accompli. 30. The Persians became aware of the aims of the Byzantines, and sought to impede their efforts in the way of expanding their eastern trade; until, when the emperor of Byzantium realized this, he sent to the Himyarites instigating them to wage war on the Persians. 31. This historian regarded the history of mankind from a western angle, and as though the pivot of world history were the west. 32. The crowds flocked to the war as though they sensed in it a more spacious and [more extreme in variety] more varied * life. 33. He apparently saw no impediment to this action. 34. It was simply as a result of the recent developments that he [changed from] abandoned * his earlier opinion. 35. There may be various views on this, but one basic truth cannot be ignored. 36. That was perhaps the most important of the characteristics of the Crusades. 37. [The mistake you are making is indeed grave] You are making a very grave mistake.

18

1. The two armies met by the city of Bira. 2. Before two centuries had elapsed those principalities became powerful. 3. The truce was concluded between the two parties for a period of two years. 4. In the years 704 and 705 he fitted out two campaigns into Asia Minor, and those campaigns were sharp lessons to the Armenians. 5. It appears that the two sides were encountering various sorts of civil disturbance. 6. Dissension occurred between the sultans of Egypt and Iraq. 7. It is one of the two basic branches of knowledge. 8. It is highly probable that these two varieties of religious feeling were found in the Arab lands. 9. The two sherifs, the sons of Abu Nami, complained to him that they were being unjustly treated, so he appointed them to the governorship of Mecca. 10. Barca and Tripoli were Turkish provinces, which the Ottoman authority governed by direct rule. 11. There is then before both of you a wide common field in which you can work. 12. Rushdi Pasha and 'Adli Pasha are the people between whom this correspondence passed. 13. [Rivalry was intense] There was fierce rivalry * between these two men. 14. On investigation, we find that both these books contain primary material. 15. Baghdad in the east, and Cordova in the west, were [each of them a pivot] both pivotal points * of the political tension between Islam and Christianity. 16. [Some of them suspected some with the most extreme of suspicions] They were deeply suspicious of each other. 17. The Arabian peninsula lay between two great empires, the Persian empire in the

east and the Byzantine empire in the west, and these empires were bitter enemies of each other. 18. That was in the year nine hundred and sixty four. 19. He died after three months, being in the fiftieth year of his reign. 20. The eighth chapter of the book contains its most important materials.

(١)

١. أعوام قليلة/ أعوام قلائل. ٢. الخطر المشترك. ٣. فكرة عمليّة. ٤. المعارك المحلّيّة. ٥. نزعة دينيّة. ٦. "أوربا" الغربيّة. ٧. العسكر الظافر. ٨. الأمم الإسلاميّة. ٩. معركة آخرة. ١٠. معركة أخرى. ١١. ظفر نصرانيّ. ١٢. الآمال القوميّة. ١٣. الإستقلال القوميّ. ١٤. أخطار خارجيّة. ١٥. المجتمع "الإسبانيّ". ١٦. حروب كثيرة. ١٧. الحملات الصليبيّة. ١٨. ممالك صغيرة مستقلّة. ١٩. الأخلاق الإجتماعيّة. ٢٠. الطبقات الحاكمة. ٢١. وثيقة مهمّة. ٢٢. الأديان العالميّة الكبيرة. ٢٣. أديان العالم. ٢٤. عامّة الناس. ٢٥. أمور الدولة. ٢٦. رجال الدولة. ٢٧. عسكر الإسلام. ٢٨. مبادئ العفاف. ٢٩. أسوار "قسطنطينيّة". ٣٠. تسليم "غرناطة". ٣١. حكّام أراضي الإسلام. ٣٢. إصلاح حال البلاد. ٣٣. تأريخ بلاد العرب الحديث. ٣٤. ممالك العالم الحرّ. ٣٥. كثرة الحروب "الأوربيّة". ٣٦. حاكم "غرناطة" الآخر. ٣٧. حكّام المدن الأخرى. ٣٨. خلفاء "الأندلس" القدماء. ٣٩. مركز الحكومة الجديدة. ٤٠. مركز الحكومة الجديد. ٤١. طلوع حكومة مركزيّة جديدة. ٤٢. أسباب ضعف الخلافة. ٤٣.

تفرّق الدولة الإسلاميّة . ٤٤ . وجود الدولة الإسلاميّة .
٤٥ . وجوب تقوية الدولة الشرقيّة . ٤٦ . ضوائف الفرسان
الصليبيّة . ٤٧ . مبدأ الحرّيّة الفرديّة . ٤٨ . قوّة
النصرانيّة "الإسبانيّة" . ٤٩ . قوّة الإمارات النصرانيّة .
٥٠ . مصرع الحضارة "الأندلسيّة" . ٥١ . ظلّ الحكم الجديد .
٥٢ . تأريخ "مصر" القوميّ . ٥٣ . إخضاع ممالك الطوائف
الضعيفة . ٥٤ . خطوة "المأمون" السابقة . ٥٥ . داخل
شبه الجزيرة العربيّة . ٥٦ . مملكة "غرناطة" القديمة .
٥٧ . مدينة "غرناطة" الحديثة . ٥٨ . قائد العسكر المصريّ .
٥٩ . عقد معاهدة صلح جديدة . ٦٠ . دولة قويّة البأس .
٦١ . عامل قويّ الأثر . ٦٢ . حاكم "غرناطة" الشديد
الإسراف . ٦٣ . تدابير قصيرة الأمد . ٦٤ . تدابير
الحكومة القصيرة الأمد . ٦٥ . حدث قليل الخبرة . ٦٦ .
مرّ الشكوى . ٦٧ . العامّة المرّة الشكوى . ٦٨ . مملكة
سيّئة الطالع قصيرة الأمد . ٦٩ . أسباب سابقة . ٧٠ .
سابقة تأريخيّة . ٧١ . سابق مكانة الخلافة . ٧٢ . عظيم
"التتار" . ٧٣ . كبار أعمال الدولة . ٧٤ . كبار رجال
الدولة . ٧٥ . بعض كبار فرسان النصرانيّة . ٧٦ . كلّ
نزاع داخليّ . ٧٧ . كلّ وسائل الدفاع . ٧٨ . كلّ صنوف
الحرّيّة . ٧٩ . مقاومة كلّ وثبة جديدة . ٨٠ . في كلّ
مدينة . ٨١ . في كلّ مدن البلاد . ٨٢ . في كلّ البلاد .

٨٣. كلّ أوامر الخليفة. ٨٤. كلّ سنة. ٨٥. كلّ السنة. ٨٦. فى بعض الأوقات. ٨٧. فى كلّ وقت. ٨٨. فى أىّ وقت. ٨٩. فى أيّة مدينة. ٩٠. فى بعض المآزق الخطرة. ٩١. تسليم بعض حصون "القادر". ٩٢. إحدى الدول الأجنبيّة المجاورة.

(٢)

١. هذه الممالك. ٢. هؤلاء المماليك. ٣. هذا الملك الظافر. ٤. ذلك الظلم العنيف. ٥. أمور هذه الدولة الجديدة. ٦. أولائك الأعداء الأشدّاء. ٧. حقيقة هذا الأمر. ٨. تحقيق هذه الغاية. ٩. خسائر "الافرنج" فى تلك الوقيعة. ١٠. مثل هذا الوقت. ١١. أمثال هذه الوقائع الحاسمة. ١٢. فى أثناء ذلك / فى تلك الأثناء. ١٣. على أثر ذلك. ١٤. بسبب ذلك. ١٥. فى أثناء تلك الوقيعة العنيفة. ١٦. ذلك النزاع المتّصل. ١٧. غاياته الحقيقيّة. ١٨. استقلالهم القومىّ. ١٩. وحدتهم القوميّة. ٢٠. خطوتهم الحاسمة. ٢١. برّه الغربىّ. ٢٢. مقاومة عدوانهم. ٢٣. عوامل انحلالها. ٢٤. ذهاب دولته. ٢٥. فى سبيل استرداد أرضها. ٢٦. على أثر عدوان هذه الحملات "الافرنجيّة". ٢٧. كلّ هذا / هذا كلّه. ٢٨. برغم كلّ ذلك. ٢٩. برغم كلّ أعمالهم الظالمة.

٣٠. الممالك الشرقيّة كلّها. ٣١. في رحلته هذه. ٣٢. نتيجة أبحاثي هذه. ٣٣. في أثناء أبحاثنا تلك. ٣٤. سياستهم تلك العدوانيّة. ٣٥. مكاتبات الصلح هذه. ٣٦. "إيران" جميعها. ٣٧. نفس أولائك "الافرنج". ٣٨. نفس هذا المحلّ. ٣٩. العرب بأجمعهم. ٤٠. جميع أعماله. ٤١. هو تاريخ عالميّ. ٤٢. هذا آخر أبواب الكتاب. ٤٣. هذا هو الباب الآخر. ٤٤. هذا الباب الآخر كثير الإفادة. ٤٥. كلّ الروايات الأخرى زائفة. ٤٦. كلّ رواية أخرى زائفة. ٤٧. الرواية الصحيحة في كتاب مؤرّخ آخر. ٤٨. تلك هي أدوار المأساة "الأندلسيّة". ٤٩. ذلك هو مبدأ انحلال دولتهم. ٥٠. هي روح الحملات الصليبيّة. ٥١. أمير "بلنسيّة" هو زوج ابنة السلطان. ٥٢. الاستحمام ضروريّ للصحّة في الإقليم الحارّ. ٥٣. هذه الآراء الاجتماعيّة سائدة لديهم. ٥٤. الآراء الاجتماعيّة السائدة لديهم معروفة. ٥٥. الضرورة شديدة لإعادة نظرنا في هذا. ٥٦. الضرورة الشديدة لإعادة نظرنا في هذا معروفة. ٥٧. نحن بحاجة إلى إعادة النظر فيه. ٥٨. هذا برغم كلّ أبحاثهم. ٥٩. لهذا علاقة بالدين. ٦٠. لهذه المدينة مكانة دينيّة. ٦١. في صحّة هذه الرواية عدّة من الشكوك. ٦٢. لهم دور مهمّ في تاريخ هذه

البلاد. ٦٣. في وجود هؤلاء خطر على الدولة. ٦٤. لسلسلة المصائب هذه آثار شديدة على الدولة. ٦٥. لنشر هذه البرقيّة دويّ عظيم في مصر. ٦٦. على هذه الحملة إعادة سيرة الحروب الصليبيّة من المبدأ. ٦٧. على قائد العسكر تحقيق غايته الاستراتيجيّة بأيّة وسيلة.

(٣)

١. أمر الملك بتحصين "المنصورة". ٢. شعرت النصرانيّة بفداحة الخطر. ٣. هذه المجهودات كلّها فشلت. ٤. أرسل إلى الأسطول المصريّ بالخروج إلى مياه "فلسطين"، خرج بقيادة "حسام الدين لؤلؤ"، سيطر على تلك المياه، قطع السبيل على سائر السفن "الافرنجيّة" للاقتراب من الساحل. ٥. اقتربت قوّاتهم في "النيل" من "المنصورة". ٦. استعمل "النصارى" سلاحا جديدا. ٧. هذا السلاح الخطير لعب دورا عظيما في الحروب الصليبيّة. ٨. انتصر أعداء السلطان في تلك الوقيعة. ٩. انتصر على جند الحكومة في بعض المعارك. ١٠. فاجأوا "الافرنج" بالهجوم. ١١. قابلت هناك أصدقائي. ١٢. اجتمعت قوّات السلطان بقوّات مصر. ١٣. اشترك هو في المعارك. ١٤. خسائر "الافرنج" قد قدّرتها المصادر الغربيّة بألوف.

١٥. أيّدهم في ذلك بعض الأمراء. ١٦. انفجر بركان الثورة. ١٧. هذا يناسب الوضع الثقافيّ السائد.

١٨. كتاب فتوح البلدان يعبّر عن دور العرب التأريخيّ.

١٩. ترتكز هذه الفكرة في المدينة. ٢٠. يتناول هذا الكتاب قصّة عرب الجنوب. ٢١. يتأهّبون للزحف إلى الجنوب. ٢٢. يتكلّمون العربيّة منذ المهد. ٢٣. النساء يدخلن في المدينة. ٢٤. سنبيّن هذا في الفصل الخاصّ بمصر. ٢٥. قد يدخل في أنفسنا بعض التشكّك في هذا. ٢٦. قد تبالغ الرواية المسلمة في تقدير خسائر "الافرنج" في تلك الوقيعة. ٢٧. عادت الأراضي المقدّسة إلى سيادة الإسلام. ٢٨. جاء الإسلام بفكرة الأمّة. ٢٩. الفكرة الصليبيّة تقوم على الصراع بين الإسلام والنصرانيّة. ٣٠. بذل "الإفرنج" مجهودا عنيفا لإقامة جسر على بحر "اشمون". ٣١. أقام إلى جانب المدينة برجا. ٣٢– هو بعد ذلك يقيم في المدينة إلى موته. ٣٣. ألقاهم السلطان في السجن.

٣٤. استرحت أنا إلى هذا الوضع. ٣٥. أثار هذا الانفجار الإسلاميّ الجديد ارتياع النصرانيّة. ٣٦. جرت معركة كبيرة عند "عين الجالوت". ٣٧. قضى "صلاح الدين" بضعة أعوام في تصفية شئون الخلافة. ٣٨. أذاع منشورا بالعفو العامّ. ٣٩. انهارت الثورة. ٤٠.

احتاطوا بهم من كلّ صوب. ٤١. نجت أمم الشمال من خطر الفناء. ٤٢. استولوا على "دمياط". ٤٣. قد أجابت المحكمة على ذلك بالإيجاب. ٤٤. هذه الأعمال رآها السلطان كخيانة. ٤٥. اشتدّت به العلّة. ٤٦. ارتدّ الأمراء إلى قلاعهم فى الساحل. ٤٧. ارتدّ السلطان بقوّاته إلى "المنصورة". ٤٨. قد يصحّ هذا. ٤٩. عمّت الثورة جميع أنحاء المملكة. ٥٠. قد استمرّ هذا الاهتمام بعد ظهور الإسلام. ٥١. زوجة السلطان بثّت قوّة نفسها إلى الملك المريض. ٥٢. اضطربت الأحوال فى البلاد بعد موته. ٥٣. وقع الاضطراب فى صفوفهم. ٥٤. المعارك تضطرم فى كلّ ناحية. ٥٥. هذا يتّصل باتّجاه التفكير العامّ عندهم. ٥٦. اهتمام العرب قبل الإسلام بالأنساب يتّصل بالآراء الاجتماعيّة السائدة لديهم. ٥٧. اتّفقت زوجة السلطان مع رجال الحاشية على تسيير الأمور. ٥٨. بعد ذلك اتّجه جنود الحكومة نحو الشمال. ٥٩. اتّخذت "اسبانيا" النصرانيّة خطوتها الحاسمة إزاء الإسلام. ٦٠. يرينا التاريخ كثيرا من أمثال ذلك. ٦١. حقّق الله ذلك. ٦٢. بعد ذلك اضمحلّت آماله. ٦٣. قد ظهر فى أعماله اعوجاج تفكيره.

(٤)

١. "القوط" الذين سحقهم "طارق بن زياد" في موقعة "شذونة". ٢. خطورة السياسة التى اتّبعتها "اسبانيا". ٣. الآراء التاريخيّة التي أرادوا التعبير عنها. ٤. ذلك الجهاد المتّصل الذى شهرته "اسبانيا" النصرانيّة على "اسبانيا" المسلمة. ٥. ذلك التقدّم المنتظم الذى أحرزته "اسبانيا" النصرانيّة في سبيل استرداد أرضها. ٦. ما أصاب "اسبانيا" من أسباب الدمار. ٧. ما أبدته "اسبانيا" النصرانية من براعة في الاستفادة من تفرّق الدولة الإسلاميّة. ٨. تحجّب النساء أمر يرجع إلى مبادئ العفاف. ٩. هو مبدأ اعتنت الدولة الإسلامية بمراعاته. ١٠. فتنة وقعت في "دمشق" صرفتهم عن عزمتهم. ١١. أنفذ فكرة جالت بخاطره منذ أمد بعيد هى تشريد كلّ مسلم. ١٢. جهّز جيشا كبيرا توجّه به إلى بلاد "الارمن". ١٣. هذه مدرسة تاريخية نشأت من جذور تختلف عن جذور مدرسة "المدينة". ١٤. يضطرم الإسلام بقوّة جديدة هى الدولة "السلجوقية". ١٥. أوفد "لويس" رسله إلى ملك "مصر" بكتاب ينذره فيه بوجوب التسليم. ١٦. قد يقدّم إلينا تاريخ "الاندلس" قصّة أمير مسلم وقع في أسر "النصارى". ١٧. يعملون لغاية واحدة هى الذود عن الإسلام. ١٨.

هذه ظاهرة تجلب الانتباه. ١٩. هناك دوافع أدّت إلى نموّ هذه النزعات. ٢٠. يؤدّى استمرار هذه الحال إلى ثورة داخلية تعمّ البلاد. ٢١. للأزمة الشاملة التى يمرّ بها الغرب أثر بيّن على الدراسات التاريخية. ٢٢. عرضت هنا إلى الدوافع التى أدّت إلى نشأة علم التاريخ عند العرب. ٢٣. هذه العوامل التى أذكت فى "اسبانيا" نار الصراع هى نفسها التى حوّلت فكرة الحروب الصليبية نحو المشرق. ٢٤. عدموا تلك الحماسة التى هى روح الحملات الصليبية. ٢٥. اخترقوا مملكة "الروم" المسلمة التى أقامها "الترك السلاجقة". ٢٦. أرادوا حطم تلك القوة التى أفسدت تدابيرهم. ٢٧. هم الذين يعترفون بخالق. ٢٨. فى الوقت الذى انفجر فيه بركان الثورة استثمرت "اسبانيا" عناصر الاضطراب التى سادت عند الممالك الإسلامية. ٢٩. العوامل التى أدّت إلى الكتابة التاريخية عند العرب تتّصل بالتطوّرات الثقافية. ٣٠. هذا ظهر من سياسة الإرهاق التى رسمها منشئ "اسبانيا" الجديدة. ٣١. قطع "فرديناند" كل العهود التى تكفل لهم الأمن. ٣٢. أثار الانفجار الإسلامى فى المشرق مخاوف الدولة "البيزنطية" التى هى معقل النصرانية من المشرق. ٣٣. "بطرس باشا" هو الذى وقّع على اتّفاقيّة "السودان" فى سنة ١٨٩٩.

٣٤. منحه ما طلب. ٣٥. سيفعل بهم مثل ما فعل أسلافهم. ٣٦. يصيبهم ما أصاب أهل "بغداد". ٣٧. لنا ما يوضح هذا فى عهد "المنصور". ٣٨. "شارلمان" ردّ الإسلام إلى ما وراء "البرنيه". ٣٩. نجحوا فيما سعوا إليه. ٤٠. تنطوى على هذا المبدأ نفس كل من عرف شيئا اسمه الحرّيّة. ٤١. هذا موقف من يقتضى حقوقه. ٤٢. بدا أمام الناس بصورة من يريد التلويح بالفكرة الدستوريّة. ٤٣. جنح بعض من أضناهم النضال إلى المسالمة. ٤٤. الطبقات الحاكمة رغم ما يحفزهم من هوى التقلّب قد ارتبطوا بأوطانهم القومية بروابط عديدة. ٤٥. هذا فى ضوء ما أخذناه على عاتقنا من مراجعة نقديّة. ٤٦. استولوا على ما فى "دمياط" من الأقوات دون مقاومة. ٤٧. وجّه إلى "مكة" بعض العناية لما لها من مكانة دينية. ٤٨. قتلوا من فى المدينة من رجال "النصارى"، أسروا من فيها من نسائهم. ٤٩. سألته عن مبلغ اقتناع الوفد بما لسعيه من حظّ فى النجاح. ٥٠. قد أسرع الدمار إلى أيّة بقعة استولوا عليها. ٥١. عارضوا أىّ تدبير شرعنا فيه.

(٥ / ٦)

١. إنّ ترك الشياب القومية أمر صعب. ٢. إنّ الحرب.

إمّا لبث دعوة الدين أو لسحق الأعداء. ٣. ولكنّ خطرا جديدا داهم البلاد. ٤. إنّ في النهضة العربية التي نراها بين صفوف الشعوب العربية لبشارة طيّبة. ٥. ترمي سياسته إلى إضعاف سلطة الخديو بل إلى القضاء عليها. ٦. إنّ التاريخ يرينا كيف جنت هذه السياسة الغاشمة على عظمة "اسبانيا". ٧. وقف "الفرنج" من بعض جواسيسهم أو الخونة على وجود مخائض في بحر "اشمون" فعبروا منها إلى برّه الغربيّ. ٨. هذا ما جرى في مصر، أمّا في "الشام" فإنّ صاحب "حلب" أخذ في تجهيز جيش. ٩. هذه السياسة تعوزها الحجّة. ١٠. أمّا "اليعقوبي" فكتب تاريخا عامّا. ١١. أمّا "دمشق" فإنّ نائب "هولاكو" قدم إلى أهلها بالأمان. ١٢. إنّ القتل دفع إليه التعصّب. ١٣. ولكن رئيس الوزارة يعنيه منصب الحكم. ١٤. لعلّ في ذلك دلائل على صحّة رأيهم. ١٥. لعلّ ما حدث من بعد يفسّر ما يحدث من ردّ الفعل. ١٦. عزم على المصالحة لعلّه يفلّ من غضب "التتار". ١٧. حتم القرار على المسلم أن يخضع لاعتناق النصرانية أو يغادر وطنه. ١٨. سبيله إلى تحقيق هذه الغاية هو أن يعيد إلى الشرق الإسلامي وحدته. ١٩. استطاع أن يمزّق جيوش الإمارات النصرانية. ٢٠.

يحجم عن أن يقطع العهود . ٢١. استطاعت "اسبانيا" أن تستثمر عناصر الاضطراب . ٢٢. نحن بحاجة ملحّة إلى أن نفهم النظريّات والاتّجاهات الحديثة فى علم التأريخ . ٢٣. هذه الضربة كفيلة بأن تقضى على كل تدبير وأهبة للقاء العدوّ. ٢٤. انتهت المفاوضة بالاتّفاق على الإفراج عن "لويس" وأصحابه وأن يسلّم "الفرنج" "دمياط". ٢٥. ولكن الأكثرية أبت أن تصغى إلى أيّة وعود جديدة ، ذلك أنّ العرب أيقنوا أنّ "اسبانيا" النصرانية فارغة الوفاء. ٢٦. سلّموا "غرناطة" بعد أن استنفدوا كل وسائل الدفاع. ٢٧. كتم الأمراء خبر موته إلى أن وصلوا إلى "دمشق". ٢٨. ثم توجّه إلى "ارمينية" ففتحها من جديد بعد أن نقض "الارمن" عهدهم. ٢٩. لقد امتازت هذه الوزارة بأن ضمّت عناصر من الشباب . ٣٠. علم أنّ جنوده سيخذلونه. ٣١. قد علمت حين عدت من "المنصورة" أنّهم سعوا لتنفيذ هذه الفكرة. ٣٢. ذكرت أنّ الدافع إلى القتل لعلّه اعتقاد سياسى قام بنفس القاتل. ٣٣. الحقّ أنّ هؤلاء المماليك قد استغلّوا سلطانهم. ٣٤. الظاهر أنهم وقفوا على وفاة السلطان من بعض جواسيسهم وشعروا بأنّ الفرصة قد سنحت لإنزال ضربتهم. ٣٥. يحسّون بأنّهم لهم دور تأريخى خطير . ٣٦. فى تلك السنة وافته الأخبار بأنّ "التتار" أغاروا

على شمال "الشام". ٣٧. ذلك أنّ "لويس" تحدوه نزعة دينية. ٣٨. هذا إلى أنّ المصالح المحلّيّة قد أصابها من تصرّفات الحكومة ضرّ كبير. ٣٩. أذنه "البابا" فى الحرب باسم الدين على أن يحكم الأرض بعد الفتح باسم الباباويّة. ٤٠. على أنّ موقف "شارلكان" من العرب يمكن أن نصفه بالاعتدال بالنسبة لموقف ابنه "فيليب". ٤١. هذا هو المخرج الوحيد إلا أن تلجأ "انكلترا" للقوة المسلّحة. ٤٢. قد تعسر أن تستمرّ هذه الحالة إلا أن يقصد هؤلاء أن تؤدّى إلى ثورة. ٤٣. هو على جانب من حسن الإدارة إلا أنّ جميع أهل المدينة يكرهونه. ٤٤. على أنّ الطبقة المستنيرة رأت هذه الإصلاحات ضرورية. ٤٥. نستطيع أن نعتبر موقعة "حطّين" تختصّ بأهمّيّة بارزة، ذلك أنها مهّدت الطريق لاسترداد "بيت المقدّس". ٤٦. وإذا فقد اعتبروا هذه القرارات ملزمة. ٤٧. رغم هذه الصعوبات فإننا نشعر بأنه يمكننا دراسة التأريخ العربى.

(٧)

١. كان هذا هو شعور الساسة "الانكليز". ٢. كان اليهود ضحايا سياسة الإرهاق. ٣. كان "مصطفى عبد الرازق" هو الذى نجح فى هذه المهمّة. ٤. يجب أن يكون موقف مصر فى هذه الحرب موقف الحياد. ٥.

شاء القدر أن يكون هذا البطل العظيم هو قاهر المملكة "اللاتينية". ٦. كان مجلس الدولة يرقب فرصة. ٧. كانوا يرسلون أسرى "الفرنج" إلى "القاهرة". ٨. ذلك أنّ "لويس" كانت تحدوه نزعة دينية. ٩. كانت "الترك السلاجقة" قد اقتطعوا معظم قواعد "الشام". ١٠. كانت "طليطلة" عند انهيار الخلافة قد قام بالأمر فيها قاضيها. ١١. كان له النصر. ١٢. كان لدسائس "الترك" أثر كبير في هذا التفرّق. ١٣. كان لدعوته شأن عظيم في إثارة تعصّب الأمّة. ١٤. كان على هذه الحملة أن تعيد سيرة الحروب الصليبية من مبدئها. ١٥. قد يكون لفترات سابقة أثرها البليغ في التطوّرات الحاضرة. ١٦. ليس لهذا علاقة بالدين. ١٧. ليس لمصر من وراء هذه الحرب مغنم. ١٨. ليس في وجودهم خطر على الدولة. ١٩. لست بمعتقد أن يكون لهذا الملك الظافر من الشهامة والكرم ما له من حسن الطالع. ٢٠. أشعر لهذا بأنّ لـ"فرنسا" عليّ مديونيّة لست أنساها إلا أن أنكر الجميل وليس في طبعي إنكار الجميل. ٢١. لسنا بحاجة لإن نصدر حكما على هذه الحروب. ٢٢. قد ظلّت هذه الفظائع تحلّ بالشعب المسكين. ٢٣. صار هؤلاء المماليك سادة القصور. ٢٤. أصبحت العهود تعارض سياسته.

٢٥.غدت هده الدولة قوية شديدة البأس تنافس الدولة الإسلامية. ٢٦.عادت الأراضي المقدّسة تحت سيادة الإسلام.

(٨)

١. ألقى المخالف إلى نيران محاكم التحقيق. ٢. عرضت مطالبهم على المحكمة. ٣. أخرجوا على الأمان إلى "فاس" بعيالهم. ٤. بذلت بعض المساعي للمفاوضة. ٥. هزمت "اسبانيا" النصرانية في "الزلاقة". ٦. هرع السلطان إلى البرج الذى أقيم بجوار المعسكر. ٧. نكبت البلاد من جديد. ٨.قد اعتبرت هذه القرارات ملزمة. ٩. قد يؤخذ عليه بعض العنف. ١٠. فوجئ بمجيء "الشيخ أحمد" واضطرّ أن يستسلم إليه. ١١. قد أسند إلى "اليهود" في عهد الخليفة "المستنصر بالله" كثير من مناصب الدولة. ١٢. هذه ظاهرة قد ترى في بعض الأوقات. ١٣. ولكنهم هزموا بعد ذلك واضطروا إلى إخلاء "دمياط". ١٤.قد توجد في التأريخ أمثال كثيرة من هذه الظاهرة. ١٥. الأمير طلب الأمان منهم فمنح ما طلب. ١٦. كانت كل هذه المعارك يفقد فيها قتلى وأسرى. ١٧. اتّصل "المأمون" برجل يدعى "الحكم بن عكاشة". ١٨. استقالت وزارة "نسيم باشا" وخوطب "عدلي باشا" في أن يؤلّف الوزارة. ١٩. لجأ إلى

قرية "منية" الواقعة على "النيل". ٢٠. بذل "الفرنج" مجهودا عنيفا للمقاومة. ٢١. يوجد فى سياسته معبّر عن مقاصد الكنيسة. ٢٢. طلب أن يقام لـ"سير لى ستاك" جنازة رسمية فأقيمت. ٢٣. طلبت الحكومة "البريطانية" أن يباح لحكومة "السودان" أن تزيد مساحة زراعة القطن. ٢٤. تذكّر "عدلى باشا" وزارته السابقة وما حدث فيها من اضطرابات وتظاهرات سالت فيها الدماء وأزهقت الأرواح واستبيحت الأموال. ٢٥. الفكرة المعبّر عنها فى هذا الفصل تدلّ على صحّة رأينا. ٢٦. الفكرة المدلول عليها هنا قد تقنعنا بتلك الحقيقة. ٢٧. ينبغى أن تنفذ أيّة سياسة متّفق عليها. ٢٨. أقاموا الدعوة باسم الخليفة المزعوم أنّه نجا. ٢٩. طلبوا شيخا مجمعا على خبرته. ٣٠. قد يضطرّ إلى الاعتزال أىّ وزير متّهم تدبيره بمثل هذا الميل.

(٩)

١. ما تقدّمت الحكومة وراء ذلك. ٢. ما زالوا يتكلّمون العربية. ٣. قد لا نستطيع متابعة هذه النظريّات. ٤. لا نعنى بذلك أنّ "اسبانيا" النصرانية لم تعرف أسباب الخلاف الداخلى. ٥. كان "اللنبى" لا يزال هو المندوب السامى البريطانى فى مصر. ٦. لم يلبث الأمير أن خلعه. ٧. على أنّ ذلك لم يمنع الوزارة

من المضى فى تنفيذ البرنامج الذى وضعه رئيسها. ٨. كانت بقيّة من التقاليد القديمة ما زالت تربط هذا الشعب بماضيها. ٩. يجب على الإنسان أن يديم البحث عن الحقيقة وألّا يكتفى بما يظنّ أنه وصل إليه منها. ١٠. لا نضال فى بطولة هذا المقاتل العظيم. ١١. عمدوا إلى سلسلة لا نهاية لها من الحروب. ١٢. الأمير لا حول له ولا طول. ١٣. شعر "صدقى باشا" بأنه لا بدّ له من أن يواجه هذه الحملة بكل قوته. ١٤. لا سبيل له إلّا أن يفرّ من البلاد. ١٥. قد لا نحصل بعد هذا الجهد كلّه إلّا على خطوط عامّة. ١٦. ليس له إلّا اسم السلطان. ١٧. ما طال عمره بعد هذا إلّا فترة قصيرة. ١٨. لا يكاد "العراق" يخلو من هذه الأمراض فى كل سنة. ١٩. ما عاد فى نيّته أن يتابع الأمر. ٢٠. كانوا يسيرون إلى فتح قواعد متنابذة لا تكاد تقوى على دفع عدوّ قوى. ٢١. أيقنوا أنّ "اسبانيا" النصرانية لا عهد لها ولا ذمام وأنها غير أهل للوفاء. ٢٢. كان فى اللجنة عدد غير قليل من أعضاء الحكومة. ٢٣. هذا غير معنى المؤلّف. ٢٤. بدون دراسة هذه النواحى يتعذّر علينا أن ننقد بحوث غيرنا. ٢٥. كانت الفكرة الإسلامية تملأ نفسه ولا يؤمن بغيرها. ٢٦.

هذا يجب أن يقدّم على كل اعتبار سواه. ٢٧. لهذا غير معنى. ٢٨. قال هذا غير مصدر. ٢٩. ما كانت المعارك التى وقعت بعد ذلك سوى طور آخر. ٣٠. لم يؤخذ عليه شئ من العنف سوى شدّته فى حرب بلاد "الشام". ٣١. ما كان فى سياسته سوى معبّر عن مقاصد الكنيسة. ٣٢. غير أنّ "فرديناند" لم يحجم قط عن أن يقطع العهود. ٣٣. أما آثار الحروب الصليبية فلا يتّسع المقام لبحثها غير أنّا نستطيع أن نقول انها كانت مبعث القومية "الاوربية". ٣٤. نصف قرن وليس غير يفصلنا عن ذلك العهد. ٣٥. كان بينهم أشخاص ليست لهم بالفقه الدستورىّ أية صلة. ٣٦. تواصلت الحروب بلا فترة إلى حين موته. ٣٧. كان لعدم وصول الإمدادات المنتظرة أثر بليغ فى روح الأمير. ٣٨. كان يبنى معارضته على عدم استطاعته التعاون مع "صدقى باشا". ٣٩. كان كل أحد ينتظر أن يؤدّى عدم قبول طلبه إلى استقالته الفوريّة من الوزارة. ٤٠. يعتقد أنّه لن يستطيع تأليف الوزارة. ٤١. صرّح بأنّه لن يعود إلى مصر بدون النتيجة التى اتّفق عليها. ٤٢. أعلن أنّه يقمعهم بلا رأفة.

(١٠)

١. اجتاحوا البلاد فى أقلّ من قرن. ٢. فعلت الحكومة

ما هو شرّ وأنكى من ذلك. ٣. لعلّ معركة الإسلام والنصرانية لم تشهد منذ موقعة "الزلاقة" معركة أعظم في حوادثها وآثارها من معركة "المنصورة" الحاسمة. ٤. كان الاضطرام الديني في الغرب أضعف منه في الشرق. ٥. إنه أشجع فرسان "غرناطة". ٦. هو من أعظم أبطال الإسلام. ٧. هذه الحملة كانت أعظم الحملات الصليبية. ٨. روى أشنع القصص عن عسف "السلاجقة". ٩. من أجمل هذه الآثار دار الكتب "الظاهرية". ١٠. اقتحم أمنع قلاعهم وأنأى ثغورهم. ١١. هدّدوا بأروع صنوف الأذى. ١٢. كان هذا أعظم عوامل انحلال دولته. ١٣. كان هذا الفعل أعظم الأخطاء والجرائم. ١٤. كانت هذه الحملة في الواقع أحقّ الحملات الصليبية بهذا الوصف. ١٥. نحن بأمسّ الحاجة إلى دراسة التأريخ. ١٦. غزا أقصى وأمنع معاقلها الشمالية. ١٧. كان "اليهود" أوّل ضحايا سياسة الإرهاق. ١٨. كانت "غرناطة" آخر معاقل الإسلام. ١٩. أتمّ عملا عظيما لخير البلاد. ٢٠. ظفروا بآخر معقل إسلامي. ٢١. لم تقع أوّل معركة صليبية في سهول "الشام". ٢٢. لذلك كان أوّل شرط شرطه ملك "المغول" هو منع هؤلاء من الإقامة بأرض مصر. ٢٣. أما عامّة الشعب فكانوا على أسوأ حالة من الفقر والجوع. ٢٤. هي كانت

أوّل ملكة كما كانت آخر ملكة لمصر الإسلامية. ٢٥. ضعف السلطان إلى أقصى حدّ. ٢٦. أمر بضرب فلوس من أردأ النحاس. ٢٧. حشد "لويس" حملته الكبرى. ٢٨. دفن تحت قبّة المدرسة "الظاهرية" الكبرى. ٢٩. كانت سلطنة "الروم" في "آسيا" الصغرى. ٣٠. بدأت سلسلة الحروب الكبرى التي عرفت باسم الحروب الصليبية. ٣١. كانت "طليطلة" من أمنع مدن العصور الوسطى. ٣٢. كان الفرسان والسادة يعارضون حرّيّات الطبقات الوسطى والعامّة. ٣٣. الموت خير ما تلقون منهم. ٣٤. كان هذا أهمّ ما اعتنت المحاكم ببحثه. ٣٥. أقدم ما وصل من أثر الشعوبية جاء في الشعر. ٣٦. الفكرة الصليبية أوسع مدى من تلك المعارك التي يسمّيها المؤرّخ بالحروب الصليبية. ٣٧. كانت جيوش مصر أسبق الجيوش الإسلامية إلى ردّ الهجوم الصليبي وكانت أشدّها وطأة عليه. ٣٨. كان "عبد الله" أكثر فطنة وروية.

(١١)

١. تحرّكوا نحو "طبرية" يقصدون مكانا به الماء. ٢. كان "صلاح الدين" قد أرسل إلى سائر الجهات يستنفر الناس إلى الجهاد. ٣. انساب الإسلام إلى سهول "فرنسا" يهدّد النصرانية وأمم الشمال. ٤. لبث "المأمون" يتحيّن الفرص لتنفيذ مشروعه. ٥.

عادوا بعد بضعة أعوام إلى "فرنسا" يصحبهم سفراء من قبل الخليفة. ٦. بدا زحف السلطان كالسيل يحمل من يصادفه. ٧. جاء إلى مصر ينفذ سياسة "كرومر". ٨. ارتدّ "الفرنج" نحو تلّ بقرية "حطين" القريبة يعتصمون به. ٩. قبل ذلك بأشهر ذهب إلى وسط "فرنسا" يزور قصور "اللوار". ١٠. خرجت إليه وفود من أهل "دمشق" تعلن خضوعها. ١١. رغبوا إليّ في الاتّصال بالرجل أعرف منه ما سيحدث. ١٢. عرفته لأوّل مرّة وأنا مسافر في "لبنان". ١٣. أدركه الموت وهو في طريقه إلى "دمشق". ١٤. زحفوا نحو بلدة "فارسكور" وسفنهم تسير بحذائهم في "النيل". ١٥. حيّاني وعلى وجهه ابتسامة. ١٦. عاد سفراء الخليفة إلى "بغداد" ومعهم طائفة من التحف والهدايا. ١٧. أسر سائر الأمراء والفرسان "الفرنج" وفي مقدمتهم ملك "بيت المقدس". ١٨. دام الحصار وجنود الإسلام يدفعون الغزاة من فوق الأسوار. ١٩. انتصر "محمد بن أميّة" على جند الحكومة فذاعت شهرته وبايعه العرب وهنا صار "دون خوان" في جيشه الضخم إلى "وادي آش" ثم إلى منطقة "بسطة" والمعارك المتوالية تضطرم بينه وبين الثوّار في هذه النواحي. ٢٠. هرع ملك مصر يعود من حملة إلى "الشام" وهو مريض في محفّة.

٢١ . هكذا يصف "كوندى" وهو "اسبانى" نصرانى قرار المحكمة. ٢٢ . ما استطاعوا المدافعة عن أنفسهم وهم عزل . ٢٣ . أما وقد أصبحت اللغة العربية وحدها لا تستطيع أن توحّد العرب فكان لا بد من أساس آخر تقوم عليه القومية العربية.

(١٢)

١ . إذا تبيّن أن الحلفاء يريدون تطبيق هذه المبادئ تشبّث هو بها. ٢ . إذا جاء اليوم الذى لا مفرّ فيه من اختلاف آرائنا نظرنا فى الأمر من جديد. ٣ . أقسم السلطان بأنه إن ظفر بهذا الأمير الغادر فإنه سوف يقتله بيده. ٤ . أنذرهم بأنه إذا لم تحصل المدينة على الأمل فإنّ "الفرنج" سوف يقتلون أبناءهم ونساءهم. ٥ . إذا كانت أمور الدولة بيد الأرذال أمكنك أن تترقب الزوال القريب لهذه الدولة. ٦ . إذا نحن أسبغنا على "صلاح الدين" أيّة صفة أخرى غير الصفة الإسلامية وإذا نحن نسبناه إلى بواعث قومية أو إقليمية فإنّا بذلك نجنى على سيرة البطل الإسلامى العظيم. ٧ . إذا أصبحت مصر مستقلّة فلا ضرر من محالفة أمّة قوية "كانكلترا". ٨ . مهما كانت أقواله من الصحّة أو المبالغة فقد كان لدعوته شأن عظيم. ٩ . وكلوا الوفد فى السعى للاستقلال

أينما وجد الى السعى سبيلا . ١٠ . سوف يكفل للناس حقوقهم ما داموا على دينهم. ١١ . لا نستطيع أن نتقدّم ما لم ندرك هذا المبدأ. ١٢ . تأهبت النصرانية للدفاع عن نفسها كلما لاح شبح هذا الخطر. ١٣ . كانت الإمارات الشمالية تنسى خلافاتهم وتحتشد حول كلمة الدين كلما هدّدها الإسلام من الجنوب . ١٤ . لو أنّ هذا عرف لأدّى إلى فرقة فى البلاد . ١٥ . سألت نفسى عمّا كان يؤول إليه الحال لو أنّ "انكلترا" لم تسلك هذه السبيل . ١٦ . ذلك كان فى الإمكان لو أنّ الحرب لم تقع. ١٧ . كانت فائدة الشعب من هذه الدروس تكون أعظم لو أنّ حوادث أخرى لم تقع فتعطل سير الحركة المصرية إلى غايتها. ١٨ . قد كان فى وسع هذه الدول المسلمة الجديدة أن تقيم سدّة منيعة فى وجه "اسبانيا" النصرانية لو اتّحدت كلمتها. ١٩ . انسابت جموع "التتار" إلى "الشام" ولولا أن ردّتها الجيوش المصرية فى موقعة "عين الجالوت" لحملت فى سيرها كل شىء. ٢٠ . "انكلترا" حمت الشعب المصرى فى الحرب ولولاها لدخل "الاتراك" مصر. ٢١ . كاد أن يقتله لولا أنّ الخليفة منعه من ذلك. ٢٢ . لولا أنّ فتنة وقعت بين أمراء "المغول" أنفسهم لاستمرّ "جوبان" على أعماله القبيحة . ٢٣ . لولا هذا النجاح لاضمحلّت شهرته. ٢٤ . لا يمكن

دراسة التأريخ العربى دون إعادة تصنيف المادّة التأريخية وإلا اختلط التأريخ بالقصص والأدب. ٢٥. حتم على العرب اعتناق النصرانية وإلا كان جزاءهم الموت. ٢٦. الحروب الصليبية صفحة من تأريخ مصر وإن كانت فى نفس الوقت صفحة من تأريخ الإسلام العامّ. ٢٧. كان يسترشد وحى نفسه وإن لم يوجد فى سياسته سوى معبّر عن مقاصد الكنيسة. ٢٨. شعرنا بهذا التحوّل السريع فى اتّجاه العامّة وإن شعرنا فى نفس الوقت بأنّ الخصومة تزداد فى نفوس غيرهم. ٢٩. كنت أعرفه وإن لم أعدّ من أصدقائه. ٣٠. لم يوفّق إلى تحقيق غايته وإن كان قد استطاع أن يمزّق جيوش الإمارات النصرانية. ٣١. إذا خذله الحلفاء فإنه لا يحسب أنّ الثورة تحقّق للبلاد استقلالها. ٣٢. يجب أن يكون موقف مصر فى هذه الحرب موقف الحياد سواء اشتركت فيها "انكلترا" أم لم تشترك. ٣٣. سواء أيّده الوزير أم لم يؤيّده فهو رأيى.

(١٣)

١. سلّم المسلمون "غرناطة" إلى العدوّ القاهر. ٢. تحمّس الجنود المصريون وأعملوا سيوفهم فى بقايا الصليبيين. ٣. أما المندوبون فقد رفضتهم الحكومة. ٤. الحقيقة أنّ المؤرّخين مبالغون فى هذا. ٥. وكل

المندوبين بالمفاوضة. ٦. وكل المندوبون بالمفاوضة. ٧.
منح "الموريسكيون" شهرا للرحيل. ٨. لم يتابع الأمر
فإنّ المندوبين قد رفضتهم الحكومة. ٩. شعرت بأنّ
علينا واجبا يتحتم أداءه للوطن. ١٠. لا نعتقد أنّ
في هذا شكّا. ١١. كان هذا المثل السيّئ داعيا إلى
جزع المسلمين. ١٢. ما زال الخليفة مقيما في العاصمة.
١٣. إذا دلّ ذلك على شيء فعلى أنّ الوزراء يرون
أنفسهم موظفين. ١٤. اعتبرتهم الحكومة خوارج خطرين.
١٥. كانت قراءة جريدة "السياسة" معتبرة إثما على
الوفديين. ١٦. هاجر مسلمو "الاندلس" إلى "إفريقية".
١٧. قد حكم على هذا من قبل كثير من مفكري الغرب
ومؤرّخيه. ١٨. ضربه بسيفه ضربة تلقّاه السلطان
براحته فشقّت إلى الذراع. ١٩. ذبح من المسلمين مذبحة
عظيمة. ٢٠. قتلوا من المسلمين مقتلة عظيمة مات فيها
صاحب "غرناطة". ٢١. استقبل الملك سفراء الخليفة
أحسن استقبال. ٢٢. في هذه الموقعة هزم "الفرنج"
هزيمة شديدة ومزّقوا شرّ تمزيق. ٢٣. يفاوضون سرّا
ملوك "إفريقية". ٢٤. استأصلهم قتلا وسبيا. ٢٥.
تستطيع الإفادة كثيرا ممّا نجد من مذاهب ومناهج
تمهيدا لوضع مناهج تأريخية خاصّة بدراساتنا. ٢٦.
أذعن بعضهم إشفاقا على وطنهم. ٢٧. كان المماليك

قد هدموا أسوار المدينة خوفا من مسير "الافرنج" إليها.
٢٨. ارتدّ كثيرون إلى "افريقية" خيفة الانتقام. ٢٩.
كان "القشتاليون" قد ساروا إلى "بلنسية" بغية الإغارة
عليها. ٣٠. غزا "الاسكندر" المقدوني معظم "آسيا"
وبعض "افريقية" حاملا معه حضارة بلاده "الهيلينية".
٣١. هرعوا متحمسين لنصر الدين. ٣٢. المؤلّفات
التاريخية لم تصلنا كاملة. ٣٣. انسابت طوائف الفرسان
الصليبية إلى المشرق واخترقت طافرة مملكة "الروم"
الإسلامية. ٣٤. نرى صاحب الكتاب يقول معلّقا على
وفاته – وكان يوما لم يصب الإسلام والمسلمون بمثله منذ
فقد الخلفاء الراشدون. ٣٥. جاء "لويس" إلى مصر
مجدّدا عهد الجهاد الصليبي يصحبه بعض الأمراء
النصارى في جنودهم. ٣٦. كان هذا الملك ذا شأن
عظيم. ٣٧. هذه الحرب لم تسفر عن نتائج ذات شأن.
٣٨. تقدمت فرسانهم بقيادة أخي ملك "فرنسا". ٣٩.
وقعت "انطاكية" في أيدي الصليبيين. ٤٠. التجأ
إلى قصر محاذ للمدينة. ٤٢. ارتدّ في قواته محمولا
في محفّته إلى "المنصورة" وهي المحلّة التي أنشأها
أبوه. ٤٣. الفكرة الصليبية أقدم عهدا وأوسع مدى
من تلك المعارك. ٤٤. أرض "فرنسا" ليست أكثر من أرض
مصر خصبا. ٤٥. مكث هناك أيّاما. ٤٦. استمرّت

المعارك المحلّية أسابيع. ٤٧. تخلّف الصليبيون قليلا أمام أسوار "طرابلس". ٤٨. نزلوا مصر لأول مرّة أيام "الملك الكامل". ٤٩. كان يبحث عن هذا الأمر مدى طويلا. ٥٠. اختار الثوّار مكانه زعيما أخر. ٥١. تتّصل هذه الدولة جنوبا بحدود "فلسطين". ٥٢. ردّ عليه الشرق بعدّة كرات كانت أعظمها خطرا سنة ١٧ ق.م.

(١٤)

١. اعتزموا أن يجعلوا من إماراتهم جبهة موحّدة. ٢. آثروا فى النهاية أن يلتهموا أشلاء الدولة الشرقية على أن يحجّوا إلى قبر المسيح. ٣. استطاع الصليبيون أخيرا بعد رمى المدينة بالمجانيق والسهام بشدّة أن يقتحموا الأسوار وأن يستولوا عليها. ٤. جازوا إلى "الاندلس" لينقذوها من خطر الفناء. ٥. بعث بجنوده ليفتحوا له الحصون والقلاع المحيطة بـ"تبريز". ٦. جهد الإسلام ليحتفظ بأرضه وسيادته. ٧. كان الصليبيون قد رأوا منذ سقوط مملكتهم فى "بيت المقدس" أن يحولوا ميدان النضال إلى مصر ليحطموا تلك القوة. ٨. كان المسلمون قد أدركوا أنه لكى يتمكنوا من القضاء على عدوان الغرب يجب أن يتحقق أمر. ٩. ما استطاعوا متابعة هذا النصر فيقتحموا

المدينة اقتحاما نهائيا. ١٠. أعلنوا أنهم لن يؤذوا
أحدا. ١١. إنّ المصادر لم تعطنا إجابة فاصلة. ١٢.
لم يكن له من العمر إلا سنوات قليلة بعد ذلك. ١٣.
لم يمض قرن على ذلك الحين. ١٤. لم ينج المتنصرون
أنفسهم من المطاردة والإرهاق. ١٥. لم يبد في تنفيذ
الأحكام أيّ رفق. ١٦. لم يستجب لندائهم. ١٧. لم
يستجيبوا لندائه. ١٨. لم ير الصليبيون حملة شديدة
بعد حملة "صلاح الدين". ١٩. لم يعد النقاش يقتصر
على كون التأريخ علما أو أدبا. ٢٠. ولكن زعماء
الكنيسة وأمراء الغرب لم يطمئنّوا إلى ذلك السكون
المؤقّت. ٢١. أما المشرق فلم يغنم شيئا من
خوض هذه المعارك مع جموع متعصبة لم تعن إلا بالنار
والسيف وتحصيل الأسلاب. ٢٢. لم تكن هذه الحقائق
المرّة تخفى على الصليبيين ولم تخف عليهم أنهم
يسيرون إلى فتح قواعد وثغور متنابذة متنافسة. ٢٣.
لم تؤدّ الحماسة الدينية في الغرب إلى فتوحات
عظيمة بعيدة المدى كتلك التي قامت بها الدول
الإسلامية. ٢٤. ولكن "جريجري" لم يستطع رغم ذكائه
أن ينفث في الأمراء تلك الحماسة التي هي روح الحملات
الصليبية ولذلك لم تثمر دعوته ولم يلبّها إلا نفر
قليل. ٢٥. ولنستعرض الآن نقاش هذا الكتاب النفيس.

٢٦. ولنأخذ موضوعا معيّنا كمثل. ٢٧. فلنترك دائرة الحدس ولنعد إلى رواية الحوادث. ٢٨. فلنستغن عن متابعة هذا الأمر.

(١٥)

١. قد يطول هذا عن الوصف. ٢. قد قصرت مدّة حكمه عن تطوّر هذه الفكرة. ٣. لقيت الديار "الحلبية" و"حلب" نفسها من فظائع "المغول" ما يضيق القلم عن ذكره. ٤. طلبوا فرصة لإلغاء المعاهدة. ٥. ولكن الصليبيين نزلوا إلى البرّ في اليوم التالي لمقدمهم. ٦. شاء القدر أن يكون "فيليب" هو المنفذ لهذه السياسة. ٧. كانوا يرون فيه الصورة التامّة لرجل الدولة. ٨. كان سقوط "أنطاكية" بعد أن صمدت لحصار دام أشهرا نتيجة لخيانة بعض الزعماء المحلّيّين. ٩. هي زوجة شرعيّة للسلطان. ١٠. إنّ "الموريسكيين" أعداء لاسبانيا. ١١. قد قصدت هذه الحملة إلى مصر مباشرة لتجعل منها ميدانا للحرب المقدسة وغنما للكنيسة. ١٢. في السنة الثانية لولايته فكر في إعادة الخلافة إلى سابق مكانتها. ١٣. إنّ الأزياء واللغة والأخلاق والعادات الاجتماعية كلها تقاليد للتربية والعرف. ١٤. اتّخذ مدينة "آمد" عاصمة له. ١٥. نفي المخالفين منهم. ١٦. هاجرت جموع كثيرة

منهم إلى "فاس". ١٧. أقيمت محكمة من رجال الدين. ١٨. جرى جهاد مستمر من الإسلام. ١٩. رأى كل معارضة من أصدقائه كخيانة. ٢٠. الحروب الصليبية فى معنى من المعانى صفحة من تاريخ مصر القومى. ٢١. كان هذا طورا آخر من أطوار ذلك الصراع العام. ٢٢. لم تكن المعارك المتوالية التى وقعت بعد ذلك فى سهول "الشام" ومصر بين المسلمين و"الفرنج" واستطالت زهاء قرن ونصف سوى طور آخر من أطوار ذلك الصراع العام. ٢٣. لعلّ قبول استقالته بهذه السرعة كان مظهرا من مظاهر الغضب. ٢٤. كانت المعركة فى الواقع فاتحة لفصل جديد من فصول هذه الحرب. ٢٥. من المنتظر أن تكون الروايات شفوية. ٢٦. إنّ من المؤكد أنّ جميع البلاد الخاضعة لحكم "المغول" كانت فى ذلك الزمان تحت سيطرة "جوبان". ٢٧. من أسباب هذا النزاع الدائم تنافر البداوة والحضارة. ٢٨. مصنّف هذا الكتاب ليس ممّن نثق به. ٢٩. ممّا هو جدير بالذكر فى هذه الفترة أنّ فلول الصليبيين الذين كانوا فى بعض ثغور "الشام" انتهزوا فرصة هجوم "التتار" فأغاروا على البلاد. ٣٠. ليس الغرض من تصنيفه هذا الكتاب بواضح. ٣١. بقيت معارضتنا له وتحدّيه لنا بلا تغيّر.

١. أتعتقدون أنّ "القشتاليين" يحفظون عهودهم؟ ٢. قلت، ألا ترى أنّ التقاء "عبد العزيز فهمي" و"سعد زغلول" يعاون على هذا؟ ٣. هل تظنّ تأليف وزارة كبيرة كما يسمّيها "الفرنسيون" أمرا ميسورا في مصر؟ إنها لمهمّة شاقّة ينوء بها من يعهد إليه بتأليف الوزارة كائنا من يكون. ٤. هل نحن بحاجة لأن نقول ان الصراع بين الاسلام والنصرانية ما زال؟ ٥. أفتسير قوات مصر المسلحة إلى جانب القوات "التركية" أم تقف على الحياد؟ ٦. على أنني سألت بعد ذلك نفسي — ترى، لو أنّ الحديث لم يكن أساسه أنه لا يؤلّف الوزارة، وكان على العكس من ذلك هو الذي سيؤلّفها، أكنت أسمع منه ما سمعت؟ أم أنّ هذا الحديث يصوّر نفسيّته الصحيحة؟ ٧. إذا أرادت الجيوش "العثمانية" أن تمرّ بأراضي مصر فماذا يكون موقفها؟ و"انكلترا" ما موقفها؟ هل تسهّل للجنود "التركية" المرور؟ ٨. ممّ ينتج معارضته؟ ٩. هو لا يكاد يدري لم نودي. ١٠. كان أهمّ ما عنيت المحاكم ببحثه هو هل يعتبر القرار ملزما. ١١. خاطبني عمّا إذا كنت أجد ما يمنعني من مقابلة الوزير وأجبته بأني لا يمنعني مانع من ذلك. ١٢. فكروا في هذا المبدأ توقنوا صحّته. ١٣. أثار ذلك نفوسنا أيّما إثارة.

١٤. قالوا له ــ أيّها الشابّ المفتون ، غرّك مركز حسبت نفسك فيه صاحب الأمر.

(١٧)

١. كان عمّي عندما وصلت من "اوربا" مقيما في "الاسكندرية". ٢. أفلا يمكن بوسيلة ما تغليب رأى وزارة الخارجية البريطانية؟ ٣. كانوا يترددون في الموافقة حتى يحصلوا على ضمان كاف. ٤. كانت سياسة "الانكليز" ترمى أول الأمر إلى قيام وزارة الوفد الأولى حتى تكون الوزارة الدستورية التى تستطيع أن تفاوضهم. ٥. ظلّت أسرته تتولّى إمارة "الحيرة" حتى استولى العرب المسلمون عليها. ٦. عزموا على الثورة على "جوبان" ووقعت الفتنة حتى كاد أن يزول ملك "المغول" لولا أن أظهر براعة عظيمة. ٧. لقيت مدينة "البصرة" منهم محن شدادا حتى قيل انهم أخذوا من أهلها ما يزيد على النصف من أموالهم. ٨. استقلّ بـ"مكة" حتى أخذها أخوه منه. ٩. أخذت الدولة "اللاتينية" تغير تباعا على ما حولها من الأراضى والقواعد حتى أضحت قوة لها خطرها. ١٠. لم يمض على تسليم "غرناطة" أعوام قلائل حتى بدأ "الاسبان" بتحوير المعاهدة. ١١. ولكنهم ما كادوا ينتقلون إلى الحكم الجديد حتى

أمروا بترك البلاد. ١٢. ما ذاع قرار المجلس حتى ذكا الهياج في كل ناحية. ١٣. ما كاد ينتهي عن القول حتى اقترب الفارس. ١٤. ما أسفر الصبح حتى احتاطوا بـ"الفرنج". ١٥. لم يمض غير قليل على هزيمة "ابرهة" حتى قامت حركة وطنية قومية في دولة "حمير" لتحرير "اليمن" من حكم "الأحباش". ١٦. كان مسرح هذه المعركة حتى القرن التالي في "اوربا". ١٧. طاردهم "موسى بن نصير" حتى هضاب "البرنيه". ١٨. بالسيطرة على "بيروت" تمّت له السيطرة على الساحل الشامي كله من "الاسكندرونة" حتى "الاسكندرية". ١٩. لما وصلوا إلى "قسطنطينية" تعهدوا أن يحكموها باسم الامبراطور. ٢٠. لما زحف الصليبيون على الشام انتهزت مصر الفرصة وسيّرت جيوشها إلى "بيت المقدس". ٢١. لما رتّب "بيبرس" أموره الداخلية والخارجية عزم على مقاتلة الصليبيين الذين لا يزالوا يتحكمون في بعض بقاع "فلسطين". ٢٢. إنّي لفي منزلتي يوما إذ جاءني عمّي. ٢٣. كان هذا الاسم "القشتالي" يحجب نسبة عربية قديمة إذ كان صاحبه ينتمي إلى بني "أميّة". ٢٤. بذلك نجني على سيرة البطل إذ نجرّده من أروع حلل بطولته. ٢٥. ولكن دراسة هذا الموضوع عسيرة إذ أن المؤلّفات التاريخية الأولى لم تصلنا. ٢٦.

كانت جميع الطبقات النصرانية تستفيد من كل أرض تنتزع من "اسبانيا" المسلمة إذ يغنم النبلاء إقطاعات جديدة وتهرع الطبقات الوسطى إلى المدن الجديدة. ٢٧. إذا "لطفى بك" يطالع الناس بمقالات فى الصحف. ٢٨. ألم يذهب "عدلى باشا" فى سنة ١٩٢١ لمفاوضة "انكلترا" والخلاف قائم بينه وبين "سعد باشا" فإذا هذا الخلاف يتّخذ حجّة من جانب وزير الخارجية البريطانية ليتشدد فى مطالبه؟ ٢٩. بذلك بدأت الفكرة تقوى وظلّ "محمد محمود باشا" يتعهدها ويغذيها بوسائله حتى إذا نضجت واتّفق الكل عليها وتحدثت الصحف فى شأنها لم يبق إلّا أن تعلن على الملأ بصورة رسمية تضع الحكومة القائمة منها أمام الأمر الواقع. ٣٠. فطن "الفرس" إلى أهداف "الروم" فعمدوا إلى عرقلة مجهوداتهم فى سبيل تنمية تجارتهم الشرقية حتى إذا علم "قيصر الروم" بذلك بعث إلى بنى "حمير" يحرضهم على مقاتلة "الفرس". ٣١. كان هذا المؤرّخ ينظر إلى تأريخ البشر من زاوية غربية وكأن محور تأريخ العالم هو الغرب. ٣٢. هرعت الجماعات إلى الحرب كأنها آنست فيها حياة أرحب وأشدّ تباينا. ٣٣. كأنه لم ير من هذا الفعل مانعا. ٣٤. إنما تغيّر عن رأيه السابق نتيجة للتطوّرات الحديثة. ٣٥. قد

تختلف الآراء في هذا وإنّما لا يجوز تجاهل حقيقة أساسية واحدة. ٣٦. ربّما كان ذلك أهمّ مميّزات الحروب الصليبية. ٣٧. لشدّ ما تخطئون.

(١٨)

١. التقى الجيشان عند مدينة "البيرة". ٢. لم يمض قرنان حتى غدت تلك الإمارات قوية. ٣. عقدت الهدنة بين الفريقين لمدّة عامين. ٤. جهّز في سنتي ٧٠٤ و٧٠٥ هـ حملتين إلى "آسيا" الصغرى وكانت هاتان الحملتان درسين قويين لـ"التلارمن". ٥. يظهر أنّ الجانبين كانا يلاقيان ضروبا من الفتن. ٦. وقعت الفتنة بين سلطاني مصر والعراق. ٧. هو أحد فرعي المعرفة الأساسيين. ٨. في الغالب أنّ هذين النوعين من التديّن كانا موجودين في بلاد العرب. ٩. اشتكى إليه الشريفان، ابنا "أبي نمي"، أنهما مظلومان فولّا هما على "مكة". ١٠. "برقة" و"طرابلس" كانتا ولايتين تركيتين تحكمهما السلطة العثمانية حكما مباشرا. ١١. أمامكما إذن ميدان فسيح مشترك تستطيعان العمل فيه. ١٢. "رشدي باشا" و"عدلي باشا" هما اللذان جرت بينهما هذه المراسلة. ١٣. اشتدّ التنافس بين هذين. ١٤. عند التحقيق نجد كلا من هذين الكتابين يحتوي على مادّة أوّلية. ١٥. كانت "بغداد" في المشرق

و "قرطبة" في المغرب كلتاهما محورا للتجاذب السياسي بين الإسلام والنصرانية. ١٦. كان بعضهم يتّهم بعضا أشدّ التهم. ١٧. كانت الجزيرة العربية تقع بين دولتين عظيمتين ، الدولة "الفارسية" في الشرق والدولة "الرومانية" في الغرب ، وكانت هاتان الدولتان عدوّتين لبعضهما أشدّ العداء. ١٨. ذلك سنة أربع وستّين وتسعمئة. ١٩. مات بعد ثلاثة أشهر وهو في العام الخمسين من حكمه. ٢٠. الباب الثامن من الكتاب يحتوي على أهمّ موادّه.